Diplomatic Recognition of Divided Nations

Yongyi Tao

Diplomatic Recognition
of Divided Nations

China, Germany, Korea, and Vietnam

PETER LANG

**Bibliographic Information published by the
Deutsche Nationalbibliothek**
The Deutsche Nationalbibliothek lists this publication in the Deutsche
Nationalbibliografie; detailed bibliographic data is available online at
http://dnb.d-nb.de.

Library of Congress Cataloging-in-Publication Data
A CIP catalog record for this book has been applied for at the
Library of Congress.

Zugl.: Berlin, Freie Univ., Diss., 2022

D 188

ISBN 978-3-631-88093-7 (Print)
E-ISBN 978-3-631-88101-9 (E-PDF)
E-ISBN 978-3-631-88102-6 (EPUB)
10.3726/b19796

© Peter Lang GmbH
Internationaler Verlag der Wissenschaften
Berlin 2022
All rights reserved.

Peter Lang – Berlin · Bruxelles · Lausanne · New York · Oxford

This publication has been peer reviewed.

www.peterlang.com

Acknowledgments

I would like to express my deepest gratitude to, first of all, my supervisor Prof. Dr. Klaus Segbers, who has supported me throughout the course of my dissertation, while granting me the freedom to develop my thesis. I would like to thank my examiner Prof. Dr. Alexander Libman for his help and advice. I also would like to thank Prof. Dr. Sabrina Habich-Sobiegalla, Prof. Dr. Sabine Kropp, and Dr. Ingo Peters for joining my committee.

Additionally, I am thankful to Prof. Li Qingsi, Prof. Zhou Shuzhen, Luong Ngoc Vinh, and Nguyen Thi Huong.

I am also grateful for the financial support from the China Scholarship Council.

Finally, I cannot thank enough my family and friends for their unconditional support and encouragement.

Abstract

It has been generally accepted that states are the most important players on the international stage, and the world by and large remains to be a society of sovereign nation-states. However, the mainstream theories of international relations take states for granted. Being recognized as a state makes a political entity a legal person before international law and an equal member in the international society. For a political entity whose statehood is problematic, recognition is a matter of great significance – in addition to a legal status among sovereign states, international recognition would broaden its living space on the world stage and justify its legitimacy domestically. Meanwhile, the struggle for recognition provides a narrative around which the state and its people could develop a distinct political identity. Especially so in the case of those political entities in divided nations, where the nation-state congruence principle is challenged, two conflicting regimes make overlapping claims to represent the entire nation. It is well-known that after the end of the Second World War, China, Germany, Korea, and Vietnam were divided into competing political entities. In the ensuing diplomatic battle, two contending regimes often claimed to be the sole legal representative of the entire nation, which makes it a zero-sum game. With the spread of the Cold War and the further expansion of the so-called international community, the recognition game concerns every state in the system. This dissertation tries to explain why a political entity of divided nations could win recognition from some states.

This research focuses on the diplomatic recognition of divided nations from 1950 to 1990. Combining the large-N quantitative analysis and in-depth comparative study, this dissertation confirms that the Cold War bipolarity played a significant role in achieving recognition from bloc members while preventing recognition of opponents. However, in the long run, the traditional effectivist principle would prevail. States in different regions also show different preferences, as the European neutrals are more Western oriented, and the African and Asian non-aligned agents more sympathetic to the nationalist and anti-imperialist cause; nonetheless they are more interested in issues embedded in their own respective regions. In contrast to some liberal argument, the diplomatic recognition has little to do with the level of democracy. Furthermore, even though stickiness to the sole representative claim might undercut its chances to gain diplomatic recognition, the practice continues. This highlights that nationalism provides the main principle for legitimization of divided nations, and recognition is not a one-way action but an interaction that reflects their self-identification. This dissertation thus helps to formulate an integrated explanation to the diplomatic recognition problems of divided nations, and an alternative perspective for a better understanding of the international system and partaking nation-states.

Kurzfassung

Staaten gelten als die wichtigsten Akteure auf der internationalen Bühne, und die Welt bleibt sozusagen eine Gesellschaft souveräner Nationalstaaten. In den Mainstream-Theorien der internationalen Beziehungen werden Staaten jedoch als selbstverständlich angesehen. Die Anerkennung als Staat macht eine politische Einheit zu einer juristischen Person vor dem Völkerrecht und zu einem gleichberechtigten Mitglied der internationalen Gesellschaft. Für eine politische Entität, deren Staatlichkeit problematisch ist, ist die Anerkennung von großer Bedeutung – neben einem Rechtsstatus unter souveränen Staaten würde eine internationale Anerkennung ihren Lebensraum auf der Weltbühne erweitern und ihre Legitimität im Inland rechtfertigen. Inzwischen liefert der Kampf um Anerkennung ein Narrativ, um das der Staat und seine Bevölkerung eine eigene politische Identität entwickeln können. Und dies gilt besonders für politische Einheiten in gespaltenen Nationen, in denen das nationalstaatliche Kongruenzprinzip in Frage gestellt wird und zwei widersprüchliche Regime überschneidende Ansprüche erheben, die gesamte Nation zu vertreten. Es ist bekannt, dass China, Deutschland, Korea und Vietnam nach dem Ende des Zweiten Weltkriegs in konkurrierende politische Einheiten aufgeteilt wurden. Im darauffolgenden diplomatischen Wettstreit behaupteten zwei konkurrierende Regime oft, der einzige gesetzliche Vertreter der gesamten Nation zu sein, was es zu einem Nullsummenspiel macht. Mit der Ausbreitung des Kalten Krieges und der weiteren Ausdehnung der sogenannten internationalen Gemeinschaft betrifft das Anerkennungsspiel jeden Staat im System. Diese Dissertation versucht zu erklären, warum eine politische Entität geteilter Nationen von einigen Staaten anerkannt werden kann.

Die Untersuchung konzentriert sich dabei auf die diplomatische Anerkennung geteilter Nationen von 1950 bis 1990. Sie kombiniert die quantitative Analyse und eine eingehende vergleichende Studie und argumentiert, dass die Bipolarität des Kalten Krieges eine bedeutende Rolle bei der Anerkennung von Blockmitgliedern spielte und gleichzeitig die Anerkennung von Gegnern verhinderte. Langfristig würde sich jedoch das traditionelle effektivistische Prinzip durchsetzen. Staaten in verschiedenen Regionen zeigen auch unterschiedliche Präferenzen, da die europäischen Neutralen eher westlich orientiert sind und die afrikanischen und asiatischen Blockfreien dem nationalistischen und anti-imperialistischen Anliegen mehr Sympathie entgegenbringen, jedoch vorrangig an Themen interessiert sind, durch die sie in ihre jeweilige Region eingebettet sind. Im Gegensatz zu manchen liberalen Argumentationen hat die diplomatische Anerkennung wenig mit dem Grad der Demokratie zu tun. Auch wenn das Festhalten an dem alleinigen Vertreteranspruch die Chancen auf diplomatische Anerkennung untergraben könnte, wird die Praxis fortgesetzt. Darin wird hervorgehoben, dass der Nationalismus das Hauptprinzip für die Legitimation gespaltener Nationen darstellt, und dass Anerkennung keine einseitige Aktion ist, sondern eine Interaktion, die ihre Selbstidentifikation widerspiegelt. Diese Dissertation trägt somit dazu bei, eine integrierte Erklärung der diplomatischen Anerkennung geteilter Nationen und eine alternative Perspektive für ein besseres Verständnis des internationalen Systems und der partizipierenden Nationalstaaten zu formulieren.

Contents

Abbreviations

ACC:	Allied Control Council
AHC:	Allied High Commission
CCP:	Chinese Communist Party
CDU:	Christian Democratic Union
CINC:	Composite Index of National Capacity
COW:	Correlates of War
CPVA:	Chinese People's Volunteer Army
CSU:	Christian Social Union
DMZ:	Demilitarized Zone
DPRK:	Democratic People's Republic of Korea
DRV:	Democratic Republic of Vietnam
EU:	European Union
FDP:	Free Democratic Party
FRG:	Federal Republic of Germany
GDR:	German Democratic Republic
ICC:	International Commission for Supervision and Control
IR:	International Relations
KMT:	Kuomingtang (Guomindang, Chinese Nationalist Party)
MfAA:	Ministerium für Auswärtige Angelegenheiten (Ministry for Foreign Affairs, GDR)
NATO:	North Atlantic Treaty Organization
NLF:	National Liberation Front of South Vietnam
OSS:	American Office of Strategic Services
PRC:	People's Republic of China
PRG:	Provisional Revolutionary Government of the Republic of South Vietnam
ROC:	Republic of China
ROK:	Republic of Korea
RVN:	Republic of Vietnam
SBZ:	Sowjetische Besatzungszone (Soviet Zone of Occupation)
SED:	Sozialistische Einheitspartei Deutschlands (Socialist Unity Party)
SPD:	Sozialdemokratische Partei Deutschlands (Social Democratic Party of Germany)
SVN:	State of Vietnam
UN:	United Nations

UNTCOK: United Nations Temporary Commission on Korea
VWP: Vietnamese Workers' Party, also known as the Lao-Dong Party
WPK: Workers' Party of Korea

Chapter 1 Introduction

There have been a bunch of predications about the demise of the state as a natural consequence of the strengthening of international governmental bodies and nongovernmental organizations, and the increasing globalization of information and economic forces. Marxism predicts that the state would wither away when the workers win over the bourgeoisies and build a classless society.[1] At the very beginning of the new century, Michael Hardt and Antonio Negri hold the view that while nation-states are becoming unable to regulate economic and cultural exchanges in an age of globalization, a global order is emerging, and it is supranational powers that rule the global system.[2] Alexander Wendt goes further and claims that a world state is inevitable.[3]

However, recent events have shown that globalization backlashed, and nationalism has been reinforced all over the globe, involving the highly developed and developing countries alike. Leading some to worry how, quoting the expression of *The Economist*, "Europe's populists are waltzing into the mainstream."[4] It is ironic to see the Brexit Party in the United Kingdom taking the lead and winning twenty-nine seats in the 2019 European Parliament elections. And the rise of populism is clearly not an exclusive European phenomenon. The singing of "Make America Great Again" is echoed on the other side of the ocean, not to mention other populist leaders around the world, like Vladimir Putin in Russia, Recep Tayyip Erdogan in Turkey, Nicolas Maduro in Venezuela, and Joko Widodo in Indonesia, to name but a few. Facts speak louder than words. Globalization is confronting challenges; furthermore de-globalization is fueled by the Covid-19 pandemic.[5] A world state is still and remains an imagination, if not an illusion. Meanwhile, the nation-state is far from dying out.

In the era of digitalization, the state will be further strengthened by new technologies. Jamie Susskind heralds the arrival of the supercharged state, which would enjoy formidable power to enforce the law, and be able to predict and/ or prevent crime in the first place. And it is very likely that an authoritarian regime could take complete control over the means of force, scrutiny, and

---

1   For a more detailed discussion, see Cummins, 1980.
2   Hardt and Negri, 2000: xii.
3   Wendt, 2003: 491–492.
4   *The Economist*, Feburuary 3, 2018.
5   Yan, 2020: VI.

perception-control, and hence make the society imagined by George Orwell in his 1949 fiction a reality of our times.[6]

From a geopolitical point of view, Saul Cohen argues that globalization "is the handmaiden of the nation-state system, which influences state policies, but not to the point that it undermines nationalism."[7] And multinational corporations remain subject to laws and regulations both in their home countries and in other countries where they operate. Other writers have confirmed that globalization poses new problems for states, but at the same time it brings with it the expansion of the authority and responsibilities of states, which means most states can do more in this era than they ever have been capable of before.[8] And as argued by Peter Lawler, most blueprints of potential world orders require the active engagements of states.[9] It is too early to talk about getting rid of the state.

What is more, the state fulfills the cultural and psychological demand of its people, providing them with a sense of belonging and identity. As Edward Said observes in the new decolonized world, to assert national sovereignty reflects the deep anxiety over the penetration of Western culture, and particularly political culture.[10]

In short, far from withering away or dying out, the state remains at the core of international relations, functioning as the most important player on the global stage. Furthermore, the international society remains a society of sovereign states.

Then what are we talking about when we talk about sovereign states? In other words, who are the members of this international society? Students of international relations might immediately respond by checking the list of member states of the United Nations. Currently, there are 193 member states.[11] But this does not include all of the earth's population. What happens to these peoples not organized in those entities making the list? Obviously, they are not living in a political vacuum. Many of them have a clearly defined territory and autonomous government, but the problem is that their motherland is not recognized as a state by most members of the international society. Recognition might not seem to be a problem for most of us, and the recognition of states has been long understudied in IR. However, recognition is important, it opens "the way for the conduct of

---

6   Susskind, 2018: 171–179.

7   Cohen, 2015: 49.

8   Meyer, et al., 1997: 157.

9   Lawler, 2005: 440.

10 Said, 1993.

11 In addition, there are two non-member states – Holy See, and State of Palestine.

diplomatic relations, recognition of passports, recognition of a nation's consular protection of its citizens, trading in a national currency, trading in state assets and debts, acceptance of state guarantees, the possibility of concluding binding inter-state agreements, the possibility of becoming party to inter-state conventions, of taking a seat in the United Nations, and of acceding to other inter-state organizations."[12] Recognition makes a state a legal person before international law. Being recognized as a state means its sovereignty is respected and under the protection of international law. The wider the international recognition a new state enjoys, the more secure its survival.[13] In the extreme circumstances, "international recognition is the magic trick that keeps weak states from sinking into non-existence in the modern world."[14]

So, what makes a political entity a state? Does recognition lead to statehood? Indeed, there has been an endless debate over the relationship between the recognition and the statehood in public international law. The declaratory recognition theory claims that a political entity would be a state if it meets the criteria of statehood, and the recognition is merely an acknowledgment of that fact. On the contrary, the constitutive recognition theory postulates that the political entity could not be a state without firstly being recognized as a state by others. Only to let these jurists and lawyers down, the practice of recognition is not a black and white issue. In diplomatic practices, recognition is a political act, conducted in accordance with the national interest of each individual actor.

For a political entity, whose statehood is in question, international recognition involves not only a legal status among states but also broadening their living space on the international stage and justifying their legitimacy at home. This has been proven in the last three decades, witnessing the collapse of the Soviet Union and Yugoslavia, and the subsequent emergence of new entities.[15] As scholars have not reached agreement on the terminological issue, these entities are called de facto states,[16] contested states,[17] unrecognized states,[18] quasi-states[19] in the meantime, while some reject all the aforementioned terms on the grounds that an entity lacking international recognition could not be regarded as

---

12 Bailes, 2015: 253.
13 Laoutides, 2020: 68.
14 Kolstø, 2006: 727.
15 Geldenhuys, 2009; Caspersen, 2012; Coggins, 2014; Anderson, 2015.
16 Florea, 2014; Pegg, 2017.
17 Geldenhuys, 2009; Ker-Lindsay, 2012.
18 Caspersen, 2012; Richards and Smith, 2015.
19 Kolstø, 2006.

a state in the first place.[20] Whether international recognition is a prerequisite for statehood has been at the center of the declaratory-constitutive debate in public international law, as mentioned before, which will be reviewed in detail later. In general, regardless of what they are being called, these entities, as described by Scott Pegg, "control territory, provide governance, receive popular support, persist over time, and seek widespread recognition of their proclaimed sovereignty and yet fail to receive it."[21] Indeed, the lack of external recognition does not render statehood impossible, but provides these entities considerable impetus to get on with their state-building and nation-building processes. As observed by Nina Caspersen, "the context of non-recognition provides a powerful incentive for building an effective entity; an entity which can defend itself and which is deemed internationally acceptable."[22] At the same time, the pursuit for international recognition provides "a narrative around which the population can build a common political identity."[23] And this is the case especially for those political entities in divided nations, where two or more opposing regimes claim to represent the whole nation at the same time.

As we all know, after the end of the Second World War, China, Germany, Korea, and Vietnam became divided into contending political entities, namely the German Democratic Republic and the Federal Republic of Germany, the People's Republic of China and the Republic of China, the Democratic People's Republic of Korea and the Republic of Korea, and the Democratic Republic of Vietnam and the Republic of Vietnam. As summarized by Gregory Henderson and Richard Lebow, "Divided nations are countries with marked ethnic homogeneity, a common historical tradition and experience of successful political unity, that have been subsequently divided into two separate political units. The division is artificial in the sense that it was imposed from the outside, usually by the great powers at the close of a war, or, in the case of China, has endured only by reason of great-power involvement."[24] Unfortunately, some writers prefer not to deal with the divided nations due to the complexity, and/or mistakenly treat them as a special category.[25] Meanwhile, under the framework of the Cold War, researchers pay a lot of attention to the military aspects of the conflicts between states in divided nations. Nevertheless, this is not the only field in which they did

---

20 Crawford, 2006; Yemelianova, 2015.
21 Pegg, 2017: 1.
22 Caspersen, 2012: 105.
23 Richards and Smith, 2015: 1718.
24 Henderson and Lebow, 1974: 434.
25 Crawford, 2006: 451.

battle against each other. The contending governments also contested against each other for recognition. In divided nations, two competing regimes often claimed to be the sole legitimate government at the same time, which makes it a zero-sum game. In such a game, a loss for one appears to be a gain for its opponent. Every third party that wanted to establish diplomatic relations with them had to choose sides: one could not have the friendship of the Capitalists and Communists simultaneously. This is best reflected by the Hallstein Doctrine. Named after the German diplomat Walter Hallstein, this doctrine is one of the most important tenets of West German foreign policy, under which the FRG refuses to establish or maintain diplomatic relations with any state that recognizes the GDR, with the only exception of the Soviet Union. The Hallstein Doctrine applied during the period from 1955 to 1969. For instance, Bonn broke off with Havana when Cuba recognized the GDR on December 1, 1963. Other regimes formulated more or less similar policies. Meanwhile, as "bipolarity extends the geographic scope of both powers' concern,"[26] as stated by Waltz, it also makes the problem of recognition every state's concern. Therefore, the competition for diplomatic recognition turns out to create more enduring tension and extensive implications.

What is more important, these divisions highlight a deep-rooted contradiction underlying modern international politics. Ever since the evolution of modern nationalism, there has been a tension between the state and the nation. The state is largely described in terms of the territory over which the authority exercises legitimate control, while the nation is defined in terms of the imagined community on which state authority rests.[27] In the ideal scenario, the nation and the state should be aligned. As Moran Mandelbaum suggests, the notion of nation-state congruency has become a leitmotif in mainstream IR theories.[28] In his masterpiece *Nations and Nationalism*, Ernest Gellner defines that "Nationalism is primarily a political principle, which holds that the political and the national unit should be congruent. ... Nationalist *sentiment* is the feeling of anger aroused by the violation of the principle, or the feeling of satisfaction aroused by its fulfilment."[29] The partition of aforementioned nations is undoubtedly a violation of this national principle. How should this incongruent situation be justified or

---

26 Waltz, 1979: 171.
27 Barkin and Cronin, 1994: 110–114.
28 Mandelbaum, 2013: 514.
29 Gellner, 2007: 1. Italics in original.

overcome? This is the starting point for every nation to re-draw the line between self and others, to re-define itself and its interests.

The research presented here attempts to answer the question why certain political entities of divided nations were recognized from 1950 to 1990. Undoubtedly the Cold War era is the critical period, as pointed out by Luke Glanville, when the discipline of IR itself was consolidated and its fundamental principles became firmly entrenched.[30] This period witnessed the competition and confrontation between the United States and the Soviet Union. Certainly, the international system was not static, and the tension between the two superpowers and their respective blocs varied from time to time. But generally speaking, the main theme was competing in a variety of areas in every corner of the world. In the matter of diplomatic recognition, it was also highly competitive since six of the aforementioned regimes had been established shortly before 1950,[31] and they attempted to justify their legitimacy over their rivals both internally and externally.

This period also covers the zenith of decolonization, which provides us with additional angles of observation. The decolonized new-born states gained widespread recognition immediately after their independence, while courted by those entities of divided nations. Even though many of them were unprepared, this was the very first chance for these newcomers to participate in the society of states as equal members. Their recognition decisions also reflect their self-identity and their understanding of the rules and principles of the international system.

Recognition is a topic overlooked in IR. The existing literature is largely qualitative, focusing on bilateral relations,[32] or a particular regional group.[33] This research combines qualitative and quantitative analysis, and it attempts to provide a comprehensive understanding about the diplomatic recognition of divided nations.

The dissertation proceeds as follows: The next chapter reviews relevant theories in the fields of both international law and international relations. It starts with the longstanding declaratory-constitutive debate on recognition in international law. For the rest of this chapter, it will examine recognition through the lens of different IR theories, including realism, liberalism, English School, and

---

30 Glanville, 2013: 87.
31 The DRV was proclaimed in 1945 but recognized by none until 1950. The RVN was founded in 1955, but its predecessor SVN was proclaimed in 1949.
32 Tucker, 1983; Obrist, 2001; Himmrich, 2016; Badarin, 2020.
33 Van Fossen, 2007; Saxer, 2017; Schaufelbuehl, et al., 2015.

constructivism. I argue that recognition is one of the most fundamental interactions in IR. Recognition is an end and a means, through which a political entity of divided nations forms and maintains its distinct identity; in the meantime, states could make use of this desire for recognition to promote their national interests.

In Chapter 3, I will further some hypotheses regarding recognition decisions, intending to provide an integrated explanation to answer why the political entities of divided nations were recognized by some states. First and foremost, the international system is considered to be influential. In the conflictual bipolar system, states would grant diplomatic recognition to these political entities belonging to the same bloc, while denying recognition to the others. Cross-recognition is only possible after the relaxation of tensions between the two superpowers. As for those neutrals and non-aligned nations, the balance of power between superpowers is likely to affect their recognition of divided nations. At the state level, the traditional effectivist principle is applied. These political entities are more or less effective, and it suggests that B_i with a larger share of the territory and population is more likely to be recognized as the representative of the whole B nation. To a certain point, geography also matters. The closer the geographical distance between State A and B_i, the more likely that State A would grant recognition to B_i. Another potential dynamism in the decision-making process is that the higher B_i's level of democracy, the more likely that B_i would be recognized, especially by other democracies. In addition, I also include national identity as a relevant aspect, mainly focusing on how B_1 perceives its relations with B_2 and its role in relation to B as the whole nation. It is expected that when B_i claims to be B, it would be less likely to be recognized.

Chapter 4 focuses on the quantitative analysis. It begins with the dependent variable and its operationalization. Here the term "diplomatic recognition" is defined as the formal acknowledgment and acceptance by State A that B_i exists as a sovereign state with an independent government controlling a given population and a certain territory. $B_{i\,(i\,=1,\,2)}$ represents the political entities struggling for recognition, B_1 is a half of a divided nation, which means that its control or assertion of control is constantly challenged by B_2. The data are generated mainly from official statements and diplomatic archives, and converted into a year-dyadic dichotomous variable. After data collection and compilation, I use SPSS to conduct logistic regression to test the relations between our variables. In general, all expectations have been confirmed. To be more specific, regression confirms that the Cold War bipolarity played an influential role in the recognition decisions of others. Standing in the same bloc would usually lead to mutual recognition. When the balance of power between the two superpowers changes, it is more likely for states to make or change their recognition decisions. As for national attributes, it could be concluded that B_i with a larger size were more likely to be recognized. Moreover, B_i were usually more likely to be recognized by neighboring or proximal states, than those far away. Meanwhile, B_i with a higher level of democracy would have a slightly better chance of obtaining diplomatic recognition. Furthermore, if B_i were committed to the idea of sole representative and insisted to be recognized as B, they would be more likely to be denied such a diplomatic recognition.

The fifth chapter revisits the historical context from the perspectives of divided nations. It is aimed at uncovering the causal links in addition to the correlations found in the previous quantitative analysis by tracing the process back, recalling the international environment of that period, and retelling the story of how these regimes entered into the international community. In the case of China, the separation between the two sides originated in the unfinished Civil War. The Communists founded the PRC on the mainland, while the ROC survived on Taiwan, and both sides claim to be the only lawful representative of China and want to be recognized accordingly. They engage each other in a fierce competition for recognition. It continues to the present day as the PRC adheres strictly to the One-China policy. Thanks to the Cold War bipolarity, the ROC could keep the title of the rightful government of China for some twenty years. As tensions reduced in the late 1960s, more and more states switched recognition from Taipei to Beijing. Due to the huge difference in size, the PRC is now widely recognized as the one and only China, while the ROC becomes marginalized. Since Cai Yingwen took office in 2016, the ROC has lost seven diplomatic allies. Nowadays, Taiwan is not "the extreme success story" any longer when discussing political entities without widespread international recognition.[34] As a matter of fact, ever since Li Denghui became president in 1988, the ROC gradually moved away from its previous position and launched a process of self-re-identification.[35] In any event, as long as Beijing firmly upholds the One China principle, Taipei has little chance to re-emerge onto the international stage as an independent sovereign state.

The division of Germany resulted from the four-power occupation and the intensifying tension between the two blocs. The FRG regarded itself as the rightful heir of the old Germany, and successfully isolated the GDR for two decades. The FRG completely gave up the Hallstein Doctrine after Willy Brandt

---

34 Kolstø, 2006: 726.
35 Zuo, 2012: 158.

became Chancellor in 1969, and the lessening of tensions between the East and West in the 1970s finally made it possible to recognize two Germanys after 1972. Nonetheless, the GDR never proved itself to be the better Germany until the end of the Cold War.

The division of the Korean Peninsula is also a creation of the Cold War. The Koreans failed to unify the peninsular by force, but only made the division of the world even worse. Pyongyang was quite successful in building up the North as a solid base for future reunification until the late 1960s, while Seoul caught up and took off since its commitment to economic development in the early 1960s. Their paths and trajectories are very different: South Korea develops via an outward-looking strategy, while North Korea becomes more isolated and belligerent. The détente between the two superpowers also affected the Korean divided nation. As a consequence, the two Koreas made some compromises in 1973, and no longer raised objection to the recognition of each other by third parties. However, cross-bloc recognition was not realized until 1992.

Similar to the others, the division of Vietnam was a result of war, but unlike in the other cases, Vietnam is the only nation achieving reunification by force. Though the DRV was diplomatically isolated outside the Soviet bloc, its resistance against the United States earned it credibility and led to its recognition by many Western and decolonized countries. The recognition problem of Vietnam was solved, once and for all, through the DRV's military victory over the RVN, and later the formation of the Socialist Republic of Vietnam on July 2, 1976.

The final chapter is about implications. Here I argue that recognition is the most fundamental interaction in international politics. It might be used as an instrument by the already established states; nevertheless it is an end in itself for the (yet-to-be) recognized. As we shall see, when it comes to recognition of these political entities of divided nations, they desire diplomatic recognition; and more importantly, such recognition should be granted on their own terms. While the practice of recognition is constructed by the international society, it is also reconstructing the latter. And the recognition decision will remain in the arbitration of individual states so long as there is no higher authority existing among and above states. Such a decision could be influenced by the given balance of power and the type of regime under consideration for recognition in accordance with each state's own interests. The international society is a society of states and a society for states.

Before moving on, as research that operates in a multitude of languages, some words have to be said regarding transliteration. Korean and Vietnamese names are used without their diacritical marks as a matter of convenience. And for Chinese, the pinyin system was applied except for some places names with a widely established English spelling, such as Hong Kong, Macau, and Taipei. In addition, the order of names follows the Eastern practices, placing the surname before the forenames, with a few exceptions where writers publish their work with Western name ordering.

Chapter 2 Theoretical Review

"The state is therefore the principle of intelligibility of what is, but equally of what must be; one understands what the state is in order to be more successful in making it exist in reality."[36]

Michel Foucault

Even in an era when the state-centric view of the world has been questioned, it remains true that states are the most important actors in international politics. To quote the famous expression of Hedley Bull, "[t]he starting point of international relations is the existence of *states*, or independent political communities each of which possesses a government and asserts sovereignty in relation to a particular portion of the earth's surface and a particular segment of the human population."[37] However, most scholars within the discipline of IR devote their time and energy to studying the interactions between states, and take states themselves for granted. Both neorealism and neoliberalism presume states as a fundamental ontological given. Neorealism shows a strong tendency to treat a "country as a whole and all that within it: territory, government, people, society" as a state.[38] For instance, Kenneth Waltz, the most influential IR theorist, describes states as "like units" because of their functional similarity, regardless of their variations in size, wealth and form, and their interaction forms the structure of the international system spontaneously and unintendedly.[39] Realists assume that states live under anarchy and strive for their physical security. At the same time, liberal theorists put more emphasizes on the security interdependence between states. Under such circumstances, liberal internationalists are enthusiastic about the formation of a liberal international order based on some shared commitment to and expectation of states, such as collective security, economic openness, international law, and institutions.[40] In short, it is about basing an international order upon the state system. Recent constructivist works argued that structure and agents are mutually constituting each other. For constructivists, the state is a

---

36 Foucault, 2009: 287.
37 Bull, 2012: 8. Italics in original.
38 Halliday, 1987: 217.
39 Waltz, 1979: 93–97.
40 Ikenberry, 2011: 15–22.

social construction; nevertheless, they generally focus on how to form some sort of order beyond the scope of nation-states.[41] All in all, IR as a discipline justifies its existence on an ontology of states and their interactions.[42]

Along the domestic/international distinction, the birth of the state is a subject left to the expertise of political scientists, who pay more attention to domestic dynamics, and emphasize the monopoly of the legitimate use of force. Alexander Wendt also follows this Weberian tradition, and defines "the state as an organization possessing a monopoly on the legitimate use of organized violence within a society."[43] Therefore the state is "initially an instrument of coercion and extraction, both against the populations subjected to states and against rivals."[44] Based on the detailed historical investigation of the formation of European nation-states, Charles Tilly and his fellowmen reach an agreement that a state is an organization which controls the population occupying a consolidated territory, it is centralized and autonomous.[45] According to Tilly, it has firstly been made clear in 1648 that all of Europe was to be divided into sovereign states, and over the next three hundred years, Europeans imposed the state system on the entire world.[46]

Such a view is widely shared in the discipline of international relations. Hans Morgenthau, the founding father of this discipline,[47] asserts that certain rules of international law were developed in the fifteenth and sixteenth centuries. In his view, the Treaty of Westphalia brought an end to the religious wars but more importantly, it "made the territorial state the cornerstone of the modern state system."[48] Martin Wight contends that the system of sovereign states originated in early modern Europe, and established itself during the epoch from the Renaissance to the Peace of Westphalia.[49] While criticizing power politics that swept the field in post-medieval Western Europe, Robert Keohane also considers the Peace of Westphalia in 1648 as the founding event and legitimation of the state system.[50] Hendrik Spruyt says of the Peace of Westphalia that it "formally

41 Wendt, 2003: 491–452.
42 Mandelbaum, 2013: 530.
43 Wendt, 2003: 504.
44 Halliday, 1987: 220.
45 Tilly, 1975: 71–72.
46 Tilly, 1975: 45–46.
47 Hoffmann, 1977: 44.
48 Morgenthau, 1973: 272.
49 Wight, 1977.
50 Keohane, 1986: 8.

acknowledged a system of sovereign states."[51] Immanuel Wallerstein confirms that the Treaty of Westphalia institutionalized the interstate system, and codified certain rules which "were elaborated and expanded later under the rubric of international law."[52] Such quotes could be multiplied easily.[53]

Grounded on such a consensus, the development of global politics could be summarized as a two-step process, which is described by John Hobson as the Eurocentric Big Bang Theory:[54] (1) sovereign states and the system explode in West Europe. (2) the system expands until it covers the whole world. The expansion of the system can also be divided into two phases: (2a) the geographical expansion, which means Europeans impose the international system on the entire globe through imperialism and colonialism until there is no *terra nullius* left on the earth; and (2b) the political expansion, which means non-Europeans, willingly or not, transform into sovereign states, achieve self-determination, and become members of the international system.

During the first phase of expansion, one could become a member of the international system through the concert of great powers. As shown in Figure 2-1, only a handful of states managed to obtain recognition from the great powers at that time. In contrast, the second phase witnessed a dramatic increase in the number of states, which came in three major waves in the twentieth century. Firstly, after the First World War, Woodrow Wilson brought his liberal ideas to the European continent, where a bunch of states emerged out of the ruins of old empires at the Paris Peace Conference. This was followed by the dismantling of the West European colonial empires after the Second World War. Under the banner of self-determination, the newly independent African and Asian countries became equal members of the international system. The third wave came as a result of the collapse of the Soviet Union and Yugoslavia in the early 1990s. Put simply, there were only twenty-three states in 1816, 59 in 1920, and almost 200 at the present day.[55]

---

51 Spruyt, 1994: 27.
52 Wallerstein, 2004: 42.
53 However, it should be noted that Westphalian principles are not fully institutionalized until the late eighteenth century. See Hinsley, 1967; Krasner, 1993; Murphy, 1996; Osiander, 2001; Clark, 2005.
54 Hobson, 2013: 32.
55 Correlates of War, 2017b.

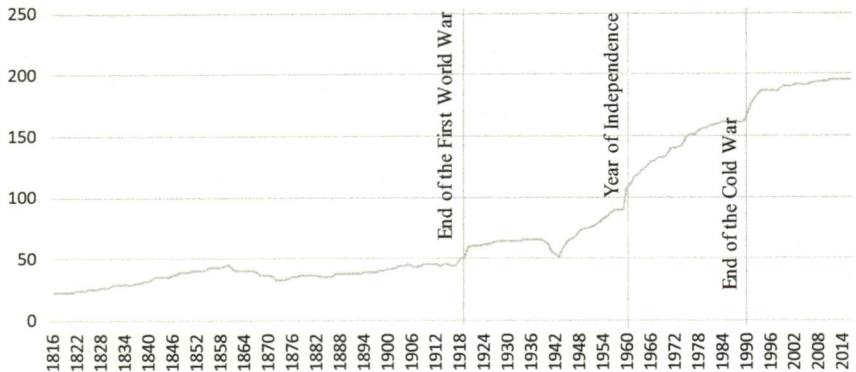

Figure 2-1. System Members from 1815 to 2016

States are not living in a vacuum, and they interact with each other. Recognition is one of the most fundamental interactions between states. As noted by David Strang, "states are not individually empowered sovereign actors, however, who *then* establish relations with each other. Rather, notions of sovereignty imply a state society founded on mutual recognition."[56] Lacking concrete definition, the meaning of recognition varies from case to case. At a minimum level, recognition means that a political entity is acknowledged to be an equal member of the existing international system of states. The great powers make use of recognition to secure their advantages. Ever since the nineteenth century, liberal thinkers and international lawyers have been working on this concept as a significant part of public international law to regulate the relations between states. Moreover, recognition could be interpreted as affirmation of status and prestige. When two political entities make overlapping claims to a certain population and territory, the fact that a third-party grants recognition to one instead of the other could be understood as showing of support, as an endorsement.

This chapter starts with the declaratory-constitutive debate over recognition in international law. This is followed by a discussion of the different interpretations of recognition. It is argued that these views are not mutually exclusive, but complementary. The state, like a person, has its own sense of self and has a psychological need to be recognized by others. Those others could make use of such a desire to increase their national interests or to promote certain norms and

---

56 Strang, 1991: 148. Italics in original.

values. To have a deeper understanding of recognition decisions, it is better to take all of these ideas into consideration.

2.1. Recognition in International Law

Looking at the expansion of the international system, it is important to ask: Who deserved recognition? For those who lived outside of Europe, this was a matter of life and death. Empirical evidence confirms that political entities that lack recognition as sovereign states are in a deeply vulnerable position. As observed by David Strang, there were 274 non-European entities that succumbed to conquest during the period between 1415 and 1987, among which eleven were recognized as sovereign states by the Western states, while 263 were unrecognized. Strang claims that virtually every community lacking recognition during this period suffered annexation or secession.[57] In other words, being recognized is equivalent to being under the protection of international law, while non-recognition could cause grave dangers. Ersun Kurtulus notes that "[non-recognized states] have a legal status that is uncertain, an international standing that is indefinite, a legal existence that is often relative, and a security situation that is at times precarious."[58]

Recognition has been laid at the center of international law. The Institute of International Law defines recognition as the act by which states "acknowledge the existence on a definite territory of a human society politically organized, independent of any other existing state, and capable of observing the obligations of international law, and by which they manifest therefore their intention to consider it a member of the international community."[59] Malcolm N. Shaw, in his comprehensive manual *International Law*, writes about recognition as "a statement by an international legal person as to the status in international law of another real or alleged international legal person or of the validity of a particular factual situation."[60] In addition, he claims that "it is not enough for the recognizing state simply to be aware of the facts, it must desire the coming into effect of the legal and political results of recognition."[61]

G. W. F. Hegel announces that "the state has a primary and absolute entitlement to be a sovereign and independent power in the eyes of others, i.e. to

---

57 Strang, 1991: 154-159.
58 Kurtulus, 2005: 125.
59 Institut De Droit International, 1936: 185.
60 Shaw, 2017: 330.
61 Shaw, 2017: 336.

be recognized by them."[62] Based on this idea, the constitutive theory of recognition has been developed, which postulates that a political entity would not be a state without firstly being recognized as a state by others. The strongest adherent is Lissa Oppenheim, who eloquently asserts that it is "through recognition only and exclusively a State becomes an International Person and a subject of International Law."[63]

The constitutive theory reflects the assumption underlying the mainstream IR theories, namely the anarchical nature of the international system. As James Brierly comments, "the constitutive theory of recognition gains most of its plausibility from the lack of centralized institutions in the system, and it treats this lack not as an accident due to the stage of development which the law has so far reached, but as an essential feature of the system."[64]

The constitutive theory has some serious weaknesses. First of all, a political entity unrecognized as a state under the regulation of international law exists in a legal vacuum and is thus considered to have neither rights nor duties in international law, and it can therefore neither be protected nor be bound by rules of non-aggression and non-intervention. On the other hand, a state is legally entitled to deny the right of existence to a political entity fulfilling the conditions of statehood by simply refusing or withdrawing recognition.[65] We could, for instance, have a look at the unstable situation in the Middle East; what transpired there did not follow the logic of the constitutive theory. Obviously, although the Arab states refuse to recognize Israel, they have never given up condemning the latter's military actions according to these principles of international law.

And things become much more complicated when a political entity has been recognized only by some states, which means it is simultaneously a state and a nonstate. This is not only a breach of common sense, but also, as pointed out by Hersch Lauterpacht, "a negation of the unity of international law."[66] When universal recognition is unattainable, is it possible to apply the majority rule as a second-best option? Then, one might ask, how many recognizing states are required to clear the bar to statehood? Clearly, there is still no commonly accepted answer to this question. Some scholars suggest international recognition be arrayed along a spectrum, with full membership in the United Nations at

---

62 Hegel, 1991: 366.
63 Oppenheim, 1955: 126.
64 Brierly, 1963: 140.
65 Lauterpacht, 1947: 4.
66 Lauterpacht, 1947: 78.

one end, and bilateral recognition at the other.[67] The subjectivity of such recognition is inherently partial and relative, and remains so, unless a universality of recognition is achieved, otherwise an extremely embarrassing confusion would persist within the international community.[68]

What is more, the constitutive theory minimizes the role of law, as Thomas Grant trenchantly criticizes, "constitutivism accented the character of states as free political actors."[69] It is also unclear whether the decision to recognize should be based on facts, norms, political considerations, or a combination of these factors.[70] From a strict constitutive point of view, recognition is a device of power politics.[71]

As a resistance to the domination of European powers, American states gathered in 1933 and published *the Montevideo Convention on the Rights and Duties of States*. In its very first article, the criteria of statehood included "(1) a permanent population, (2) a defined territory, (3) government, and (4) capacity to enter into relations with the other states."[72] This definition of the state, albeit not satisfactory to everyone, is considered to be the "best known formulation of the basic criteria for statehood."[73] The *Montevideo Convention* further declared that "the political existence of the state is independent of recognition by the other states."[74] Accordingly, recognition of a state is no more than an official confirmation of its existence, the European powers should no longer determine the others' political existence and membership in the international system by their act of recognition. Put another way, recognition does not create a state but presupposes a state's existence.[75] This sort of view is known as the declarative theory of recognition.

Founded on the principal of territoriality and the effectiveness of government, the declaratory theory is considered the dominant – even the better – theory in international law scholarship.[76] Ryngaert and Sobie argue that the declaratory theory "deprives the states of the prerogative of deciding on statehood based on political arbitrariness, in favor of objective legal norms."[77] And it is therefore

---

67 Shelef and Zeira, 2017: 538.
68 Chen, 1951: 39–40.
69 Grant, 1999: 3.
70 Ryngaert and Sobrie, 2011: 469.
71 Peterson, 1982: 325–326; Grant, 1999: 3.
72 Montevideo Convention, 1933.
73 Crawford, 2006: 36.
74 Montevideo Convention, 1933.
75 James, 1986: 147.
76 Fabry, 2010: 4; Sterio, 2013: 48; Shaw, 2017: 331.
77 Ryngaert and Sobrie, 2011: 470.

understandable that relatively young states and new governments are more likely to support such a declaratory view, and the interwar period and the Cold War era witnessed the wide application of this theory.

If the declaratory theory holds true, there would be virtually no consequences of recognition or non-recognition at all, and the newcomers would have no need to worry about acquiring the desired international status among their peers.[78] But, what if the candidates make overlapping claims to some particular territory and population? There is a tendency that the recognizing states should make decisions based on objectiveness, namely what is under whose effective control. However, following the principle of effectiveness, the statehood of microstates will be problematic. For instance, the Vatican City is the smallest sovereign state, with a minuscule territory of 0.44 km^2 in the heart of Rome, and a population of 1000 which does not increase naturally, and it relies upon Italy for basic services. James Crawford criticizes that "the criteria for statehood in its case are only marginally (if at all) complied with."[79]

Moreover, one would ask, is a self-proclaimed state indeed already a state? If the declaratory theory is correct, then what about the Islamic State? Does it mean that as Abu Bakr al-Baghdadi announced the establishment of the Islamic State, its statehood followed from that declaratory act immediately? Are those states, who indirectly supporting or are actively engaged in fighting the Islamic State, invading the Islamic State, and violating its sovereignty? Andrew Coleman rightfully argues that the emergence of the Islamic State raises a series of fundamental issues in international law, including not only the concepts of state, of recognition, but also those of humanitarian intervention and the use of force.[80]

Therefore, recognition is considered to have constitutive effects indeed. Shaw admits that recognition is constitutive in the sense that "it marks the new entity out as a state within the international community and is evidence of acceptance of its new political status by the society of nations."[81] Yet, as noted by Onuf, "no one act of recognition suffices for constitutive purpose, for the performance of such an act would effectively shift agency from the aggregate of governments to one in particular."[82]

---

78 Vidmar, 2009: 828.
79 Crawford, 2006: 223.
80 Coleman, 2014: 75–80.
81 Shaw, 2017: 323.
82 Onuf, 1994: 17.

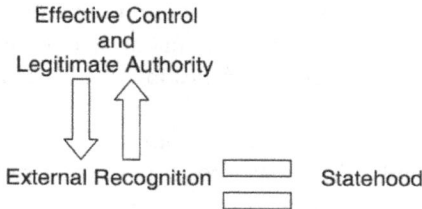

Figure 2-2. Two Models of State Emergence. Coggins (2014: 29)

In a nutshell, neither the declaratory nor the constitutive theory is satisfactory. Recognition is not clear-cut along this declaratory-constitutive dichotomy (see Figure 2-2). Ian Brownlie complained some thirty years ago that "in the case of 'recognition' theory has not only failed to enhance the subject but has created a *tertium quid* which stands, like a bank of fog on a still day, between the observer and the contours of the ground which calls for investigation."[83] And after his study on state recognition, Grant concludes that the theory of recognition has become less and less illuminating, while the fog observed "has not lifted but in fact has thickened."[84] After all, as he rightfully asserts, international law is made by states through their practice.[85]

2.2. Recognition in Power Politics

As reflected in the debate among international law scholars, the proliferation of the application of the term state without certain rules is problematic. For realists, such rules are determined by the self-interest of the recognizing states. As mentioned before, the realist theory is constructed on the Westphalian model of sovereignty, and takes the state as the main actor, which is presumed to be an

---

83 Brownlie, 1983: 627.
84 Grant, 1999: ix.
85 Grant, 1999: 218.

ontological given. States interact in a decentralized and anarchic system, where the international structure is defined by the primary actors and the distribution of capabilities across them.[86] Lacking an overarching ruler, states make their own decisions about whether to recognize an entity, or to deny recognition to it. For power-maximizing states, recognition is no more than a part of the foreign policy tool kit. The international state system expands but also unintentionally destabilizes itself at the same time by such practice. This kind of destabilization is an almost inevitable consequence as newcomers' entries into the system are contingent on political considerations.[87]

Unlike international lawyers denouncing politically motivated recognition decisions, M. J. Peterson frankly admits that "any recognition policy can be viewed as 'politically motivated.'"[88] Even those who endorse strict recognition policy on the basis of effectiveness will eventually gain from having such an order accepted as the norm. In general, he accepts the use of recognition of governments as a political tool to secure their unilateral advantages, which can be categorized as taking three distinct forms: "(1) expressing approval or disapproval of a particular new regime or its methods of taking power, (2) influencing the new regime's policies by trading recognition for concessions, and (3) affecting the choice of government in another state by encouraging or discouraging the new regime or different factions in an ongoing civil war."[89] The importance and effectiveness also wax and wane in accordance with changing international environments and the relative strength of both the initiator and target government as well, great powers might fail to achieve their goals, as the Americans experienced in the Southeast Asia, while weak states have the opportunity to generate benefits, as the African countries' exploits of the Hallstein Doctrine during the 1960s has shown.

Peterson has also examined how the international system impacts the institution of recognition of governments and concluded that "the pattern of political use has been most sensitive to changes in the pattern of great power conflict and the level of international competition among adherents of rival political ideologies."[90] And he notes that as long as the international system remains anarchical, each government will continue to determine the status of new regimes on its own will.

---

86 Waltz, 1979: 99–101.
87 Coggins, 2014: 10.
88 Peterson, 1997: 154.
89 Peterson, 1997: 155.
90 Peterson, 1997: 187.

This view is further explored by some recent studies. After examining their recognition practice in the twentieth century, Bridget Coggins concludes that the great powers "routinely pursued their own interests where the recognition of new states was concerned."[91] According to her study, those interests include geostrategic security, domestic security, and systemic stability.[92]

Milena Sterio claims that recognition of state is closely linked to power politics, and powerful states often choose whether or not to recognize an aspiring state according to their own geopolitical interests, or the interests of their close allies, instead of an analysis of the legal criteria of statehood. Meanwhile, great powers are also able to influence the recognition decision of other states, even to dissuade the latter from recognizing an entity, when doing so would benefit them.[93]

2.3. Collective Recognition

There has been a long tradition of recognizing new states through international conferences and signing treaties ever since the Treaty of Westphalia. In the twentieth century, the founding of international organizations brought new impetus.

After the First World War, aspirant states sought not only to participate in the Peace Conference of Paris, but also requested to be admitted to the League of Nations as an international birth certificate. For instance, the Principality of Liechtenstein demanded "admission into the League of Nations so as to obtain international recognition of the sovereign rights of the Prince."[94] This is further illustrated by similar efforts of the succession states to the former Russian Empire. Graham concludes that "recognition is accomplished through admission, that recognition being valid even against the will of states opposing admission,"[95] albeit "the principle of automatic recognition through admission will gain general validity only when the League becomes all-inclusive and its law becomes international law."[96] Unfortunately, the League of Nations failed to achieve this level of universality.

---

91 Coggins, 2014: 220.
92 Coggins, 2014: 44–45.
93 Sterio, 2020: 85–86.
94 Quote in Graham, 1933: 9. It should be noted that the application of Liechtenstein was rejected on the grounds that it was considered unable to observe its obligations.
95 Graham, 1933: 39.
96 Graham, 1933: 41.

Contemporary writers emphasize the significant role that the United Nations plays in the recognition of states.[97] As early as 1951, Chen envisages that "[w]hen the United Nations shall have attained complete universality, the notion of 'recognition' will wither away, and membership of the United Nations will be the sole standard of relations between States."[98] According to Dugard, the collective recognition through the United Nations remedies serious weaknesses of the constitutive theory: If all members of the United Nations recognize each other's existence as states, then the controversial situation of an entity being a state for some but not for others will no longer occur. Furthermore, the existence of a state is decided upon by member states acting collectively in the United Nations, thus freed from the arbitrariness of any one state's individual decision.[99] And nowadays as the member states numbered 193 after the admission of South Sudan on July 14, 2011, it is widely accepted that "admission to full UN membership is tantamount to collective de jure recognition."[100] In other words, "membership in the United Nations confers and sustains membership in international society."[101]

However, there is still a gap between scholars' expectations and diplomats' practice. *The Charter of the United Nations* has set the rules concerning the admission of new members in Article 4: "1. Membership in the United Nations is open to all other peace-loving states which accept the obligations contained in the present Charter and, in the judgment of the Organization, are able and willing to carry out these obligations. 2. The admission of any such state to membership in the United Nations will be effected by a decision of the General Assembly upon the recommendation of the Security Council."[102]

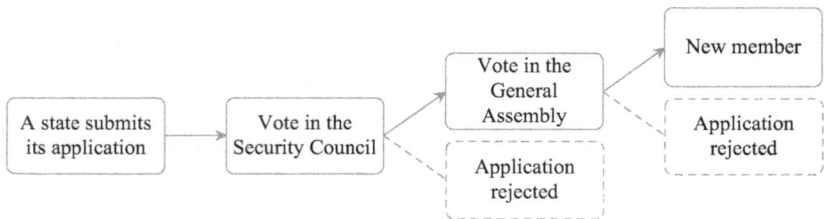

Figure 2-3. Admission of New Members into the United Nations

---

97   Claude, 1966; Dugard, 1987; Grant, 2009.
98   Chen, 1951: 222.
99   Dugard, 1987: 80.
100 Geldenhuys, 2009: 22.
101 Onuf, 1994: 18.
102 United Nations, 1945.

On each voting procedure (see Figure 2-3), member states vote according to their own national interests. While theoretically the General Assembly could reject a Security Council recommendation, it has never done so. Even as it is made up of nearly all the states in the world, the assembly appears to have limited capability to influence world politics. It is, however, influential in a more indirect way, unlike a legislature in a national political system.[103] The debate over applicants' eligibility mainly takes place in the Security Council. There, the decisions of the five permanent members are extremely critical since they can veto any application they dislike. Thus, the Security Council plays the role of a gatekeeper.[104] It is understandable that member states prefer to preserve the right to extend recognition of their own instead of transferring that prerogative to any superior international institution. Things remain the same, as the then representative of Argentina had blatantly pointed out some seventy years ago – decisions are made on the basis of political criteria.[105]

If collective recognition is not feasible on a global scale, then how about at regional level? Indeed, there are several successful cases of regional collective recognition. Immediately after the Cold War, facing the breakup of the Soviet Union and of Yugoslavia, the European countries quickly responded by recognizing the newly (re-)constituted republics. On December 16, 1991, the European Commission published an instructive document on this issue, namely *The Guidelines on the Recognition of New States in Eastern Europe and in the Soviet Union*.[106] Such a scenario encourages the idea of collective recognition, and it seems to be workable, at least at the European regional level. Some scholars argued that the role that the international society played in recognition had increased and that there would ultimately come to a time for a collective recognition process.[107]

These believers would be disappointed after closer scrutiny of the European Union's practices of recognition. In a more recent study, Newman and Visoka explore the EU's practices since 1990. Facing 37 entities seeking international recognition, the EU granted collective recognition to twenty-six states, withheld collective recognition from nine, and left the recognition problem to its

---

103 Peterson, 2006: 90–118.
104 Griffiths, 2017: 180.
105 United Nations, 1950.
106 European Community: Declaration on Yugoslavia and on the Guidelines on the Recognition of New States, 1992.
107 Grant, 1999.

individual members in two specific cases. The differentiated approach to state recognition revealed inconsistencies and internal tensions within the EU. At the same time, there also existed tensions between the EU's normative commitments, its commitment to an international order based upon the Westphalian sovereign system, and its geopolitical interests. Therefore, they concluded that a uniform EU policy on recognition would not be achieved and its practice would continue to be determined on a case-by-case basis, even though "a more coherent recognition policy would provide clarity and credibility to the EU and expand its external influence."[108] In short, the EU countries have not been able to unify their recognition decisions. There is still a long way to go before they can truly speak with a single voice.

While collective recognition is not well regulated in either international law or international politics, there have been rather strong normative and legal provisions set in place which require non-recognition of situations under certain circumstances since the twentieth century. Non-recognition has been justified as a sanction against an illegal foundational act. A well-known example is Manchukuo – the League of Nations adopted a resolution on March 11, 1932 that the establishment of the new State of Manchukuo by Japanese aggressors was a situation that warranted non-recognition. The League failed to secure a total non-recognition of Manchukuo; nevertheless, it should be seen as a precedent for collective non-recognition of a situation that has been created contrary to a fundamental rule of international law.[109] Thus, while the effectiveness of non-recognition might be questioned, the doctrine of non-recognition is intended to ensure that law-breakers are not rewarded. The rationale is that there are certain higher norms essential to the international system with which states are required to comply.

2.4. Standard of Civilization

Analyzing the historical encounter of the Europeans with the rest of the world with the help of the tools of sociology, writers of the English School focus on the process by which the international society originated from the shared practices developed among European states, and then expanded globally.[110] The expansion of international society happened in two ways, as summarized by Barry

---

108 Newman and Visoka, 2018: 785.
109 Turns, 2003.
110 Bull and Watson, 1984; Gong, 1984; Watson, 1992.

Buzan: "by the imperial absorption of much of the non-West into European empires, and by the phased admission of a few non-colonised states into international society once they were deemed 'civilised.'"[111]

During their encountering and conquering process of the rest of the globe, the Europeans formed their own identity, and also gained a sense of superiority. It is civilization, "defined by criteria such as 'humanity', 'law' and 'social mores', seemed to supplant religion in Europe's external differentiation from non-European communities."[112] In this process, particularly after the industrial revolution, the Europeans became increasingly convinced of the superiority of their own civilization. In their eyes, "modern civilization was synonymous with European ways and standards, which it was their duty and their interest to spread in order to make the world a better and safer place."[113] They developed the concept of the standard of civilization to legitimize their claim of a higher political standing and privileged legal status, to justify their colonial practices, and to gate-keep the membership in the expanding international system.[114] The standard of civilization, as defined by Gerrit Gong, "is an expression of the assumptions, tacit and explicit, used to distinguish those that belong to a particular society from those that do not."[115]

There has never been a specific set of requirements for the standard of civilization. In Buzan's view, it is/was about modernity, and "[s]o long as modernity continues to evolve, so the criteria for meeting the 'standard of civilization' will change, probably becoming increasingly demanding."[116] In general, as summarized by David Fidler, "to engage fully in international relations, your behavior has to conform to expectations, policies, and rules established by the prevailing powers."[117] So-called Barbarians and semi-civilized groups that failed to comply with these relevant requirements were barred from the international society of states, or in the nineteenth-century discourse, the family of civilized nations.[118] Yongjin Zhang asserts that "unless and until admitted by the original members, non-European states could not take their place in the Family of Nations."[119]

---

111 Buzan, 2014: 578.
112 Neumann and Welsh, 1991: 340.
113 Watson, 1984: 27.
114 Gong, 1984; Buzan, 2014; Ringmar, 2014; Linklater, 2016.
115 Gong, 1984: 3.
116 Buzan, 2014: 580-581.
117 Fidler, 2000: 389.
118 Linklater, 2016.
119 Zhang, 1991: 5.

A state is not an equal member of the international system until it is recognized as such by the Europeans – as in the case of America and Russia – and later the West.

Strongly associated with colonialism, the standard of civilization was perceived as a part of an unjust system of exploitation and domination. For sure, the nineteenth-century international system was unequal; however, the standard of civilization as the criterion for recognition opened the gate for non-Europeans to enter this club of sovereign states. In short, through practices of recognition, the international society expanded itself throughout the whole world. The term gradually fell out of use ever since the First World War, during which the Europeans described each other as barbarian, and the distinction between a civilized Europe and a barbaric Other unraveled. There has been growing criticism of the use of any optional criteria other than effective control on which to base decisions about whether to recognize or not.[120] It was emphatically asserted by Lassa Oppenheim in 1937 that "religion, or the controversial test of degree of civilization have ceased to be, as such, a condition of recognition of statehood."[121] Furthermore, Oppenheim used to define international standards as "the body of customary and conventional rules which are considered legally binding by civilized States in their intercourse with each other" in the first edition of his book in 1905, but the word "civilized" is no longer used since the 1955 eighth edition.[122] What is more, decolonization makes membership in the international society almost universal and unconditional. Anti-colonialists use a moral-based discourse to counter-attack Western efforts to prolong their colonial rules. Thus, the colonized peoples are entitled to self-determination and immediate recognition.[123]

Although the phrase "standard of civilization" fell out of use due to its close connection with colonialism, the practice continues under different terms, varying from human rights, good governance and development to democracy.[124] And Xiaoming Zhang points out that regardless of the name used, the standard of civilization, new standard of civilization, the standard of modernity or

---

120 Peterson, 1997: 72.
121 Quoted in Zhang, 1991: 7. Gerrit Gong also writes in detail about how the standard of civilization becomes irrelevant in international law during the first half of the twentieth century, see Gong, 1984: 81–90.
122 For a detailed examination on Oppenheim's use of "civilized" see Gong, 1984: 81–86.
123 Patil, 2008.
124 Hobson, 2008; Clark, 2009; Zarakol, 2011; Stivachtis, 2015.

whatsoever, they are "self-conscious attempts to create a tiered or hierarchical international society, constituted by a core and a periphery, or more loosely by insiders and outsiders."[125] This is inconsistent with the notion of state sovereignty and the virtues of pluralism in international society.[126]

Still, there are some writers who argue that there is a need "to appreciate the importance of the idea of civilization not merely as a standard for regulating the entry of new states in international society, but also for validating an entirely different set of legal rules and political institutions in its own right."[127] Such is at least a bold challenge to political correctness, if not an instrinsic discrimination against all non-Western peoples.

2.5. Struggle for Recognition

Constructivists perceive recognition from a different perspective, highlighting its explanatory value by describing recognition as a psychological need. From the constructivist point of view, recognition is an end in itself. Unlike realists who interpret the logic of anarchy as the struggle for security, Alexander Wendt argues that "the logic of anarchy is also about a struggle for recognition."[128] In other words, states seek not only physical security but also ontological security.[129] The scholarly literature on ontological security has been rapidly developed in recent decades, stressing that "states care as much about their ontological security, the security of a consistent self, as about material, physical security, the traditional purview of IR inquiry."[130]

According to constructivists, it is through recognition by the Other, and only through recognition, that one can become a Self and maintain their distinct identity. Wendt claims that the desire for recognition might not always trump that for security. Nevertheless, recognition, as a precondition for genuine subjectivity, "is part of what makes security worth having in the first place."[131] Erik Ringmar goes further and claims that questions regarding a state's identity are more fundamental than those regarding its interests.[132] Thus, it is the mutual

---

125 Zhang, 2010: 240.
126 Clark, 2009: 581.
127 Keene, 2002: 117.
128 Wendt, 2003: 510.
129 Mitzen, 2016: 341.
130 Subotić, 2016: 613–614.
131 Wendt, 2003: 514.
132 Ringmar, 2002: 116–119; Ringmar, 1996: 439–466.

recognition of sovereignty by European states in 1648 which constituted each of them individually as a distinct subject in international law and constituted them collectively as members of a society of states. In short, subjectivity is gained via mutual recognition.

Through practice of mutual recognition and building of collective identity, Wendt proposes a road map to a Weberian world state by creating a Hegelian one. However, it remains arguable whether the Hegelian mutual recognition process will continue to operate beyond state boundaries and eventually end up in an overarching world state. Neither observing contemporary international politics nor the sampling of empirical studies in social psychology could provide solid evidence for the inevitability of Wendt's world state.[133] The international system remains within the so-called "Lockean culture of anarchy."[134] Nonetheless, the constructivist IR scholars have reached a consensus at the minimal level that recognition is an end in itself, and it matters to international politics because it represents the means by which political entities become states within the international system and take on a particular identity within that system.[135]

In addition, Wendt distinguishes two kinds of recognition: (1) thin recognition, which means being acknowledged as an independent subject within a community of law, and (2) thick recognition, which is about being respected for what makes oneself special. The struggle for thick recognition is open-ended and never-ending; it could take on numerous forms varying from the pursuit of great power status to the claim of being God's chosen people. While asymmetric recognition generates tension and conflicts among actors, mutual recognition leads to collective identity.[136] This is helpful in understanding the recognition of political entities of divided nations. These entities seek not only to be each acknowledged as an independent state within the international community, but also to having their nationalist proclamation justified by the outside world. Here, thin and thick recognition intertwine. Therefore, the competition for recognition continues so long as there are rivalries straddling the iron/bamboo curtain. The struggle for recognition causes constant tensions among rival authorities.

---

133 Greenhill, 2008.
134 Wendt, 1999: 279–297.
135 Greenhill, 2008.
136 Wendt, 2003: 511–512.

2.6. Summary

To sum up, recognition refers to the acknowledgment by a state that another political entity exists as a state. It is an act by which the recognizing state acknowledges the existence of the (to-be) recognized state and demonstrates its intention to generate both legal and political ties.

Recognition is of great significance to the international system of sovereign states. A political entity thus recognized becomes an equal member of the system in the legal sense. The declaratory-constitutive debate over the relationship between recognition and statehood is akin to a chicken-and-egg conundrum. Looking at history, while states in earlier periods might simply declare their existence without too many concerns over recognition, it is hard to deny its importance in the modern age. And as a consequence of the anarchical character of the international system, it is an impossible mission to attempt to regulate the recognition practices of individual sovereign states under commonly accepted principles of international law. As Ringmar asserts: "far more fundamentally, recognition plays a role in establishing the conditions that make international law possible in the first place."[137]

Through recognition, the system reproduces itself, and the state forms its distinct identity. The struggle for recognition should be interpreted as one of the core motivational dynamics of international politics.[138] It is exactly this desire to be recognized as a state among states, and the dynamic it sets up, that increases the established states' leverage on the international stage. In order to be recognized as a state, the would-be state has to live up to certain expectations of their recognizing peers. Meanwhile, the established states make use of this opportunity to boost their own interests. It is under these circumstances that granting or withholding recognition becomes a foreign policy instrument as understood by the realists. This is clearly in contradiction of an ordered, structured procedural modus operandi of international relations as envisaged by international lawyers, a situation wherein the established states feel no obligation to grant recognition to the newcomers, legal criteria of statehood constitute only a minor part of their recognition narratives and are only just mentioned in order to defend their recognition decisions. As Badarin concludes aptly, recognition decision is usually framed as a prudent measure in the national interest of the recognizer.[139]

---

137 Ringmar, 2012: 9.
138 Haacke, 2005: 194.
139 Badarin, 2020: 91.

Therefore, the different views of recognition from different IR theories are not mutually exclusive, but complement one another. In any case, recognition as a topic in itself should not be overlooked.

With an increasing emphasis on the centrality of recognition, writers of international relations have become more interested in this issue in recent years. And recent IR studies also confirm that the great powers exercise their recognition prerogatives based on their own interests, instead of an analysis of whether the aspiring entity satisfies the legal criteria.[140]

It is the purpose of this dissertation to explore what underlies the diplomatic recognition of divided nations. As the international system expanded to cover the entire world, recognition is no longer an issue limited to the great powers. Every state has to choose a side and make its own decision, especially when the rivalry of two entities brings the issue right up to its doorstep. Instead of focusing on a handful of powers, this research is designed to formulate a comprehensive understanding, covering states of all kinds, whether they are well-established or newly independent, large or small, developed or underdeveloped, open or closed.

---

140 Coggins, 2014: 220; Sterio, 2020: 82.

Chapter 3 Hypotheses

In the previous chapter, recognition is reviewed at a macro level. Grand theories are parsimonious, they provide us with general frameworks for understanding what is going on. However, they mostly focus on "big and important things,"[141] hence overlook the minor, presumed trivial foreign policy decisions. To bridge the gap from macro theories to the details of specific policy makings, I will proceed to further some hypotheses regarding recognition decisions, from the international level of analysis to the state level and below. It is aimed at providing an integrated explanation for the diplomatic recognition of divided nations.

3.1. International System

The divisions of China, Germany, Korea, and Vietnam reflected the front line of the Cold War. Backed by opponent superpowers respectively, the diplomatic competition between political entities in a divided nation during that era was also a part of the global campaign between the United State and the Soviet Union. As both the Americans and the Soviets clearly acknowledged that there was no hope to transform the competitor in the short term, the Cold War was marked by the competition to win new adherents over to one or the other bloc. As David Engerman points out, "the story of the Cold War was the story of boundaries, establishing the outer limits of each sphere of influence and competing for those who had not yet pitched their tents in one camp or the other."[142] Everything was viewed through this lens, and so was the recognition issue of their smaller partners.

Certainly, both the United States and the Soviet Union understood very well the importance of recognition. French recognition and support of American independence was so decisive that Mikulas Fabry blankly points out the historic irony that Louis XVI was in effect a founding father of the United States.[143] Such an experience recurred in a different form during the American Civil War, as President Lincoln was aiming at defeating the South on the battlefield and preventing it from obtaining international recognition – the single most significant Confederate foreign policy goal, as argued by Howard Jones, "recognition

---

141 Waltz, 1986: 329.
142 Engerman, 2010: 33.
143 Fabry, 2010: 35–36.

of the Confederacy would provide a tremendous boost to its morale by opening military and commercial avenues throughout Europe. Southern secession would achieve legitimacy, necessarily meaning that the Union had lost its permanency."[144] Likewise, the Soviet Union has always been participating in recognition games, first in the 1920s in seeking recognition as a legitimate state, then in the 1930s and 1940s as a great power, and later during the Cold War as a superpower.[145] They knew only too well from their own experience. Therefore, the two superpowers not only took the lead to grant recognition to their respective partners, but also made strenuous efforts to coordinate recognition among their allies.

The United States and the Soviet Union divided their blocs so clearly, the ontological contrast was so stark, that they could hardly allow any misreading or manipulation. As observed by Peterson, "recognition decisions of a hegemonial [sic] power would affect those of all others, and that the hegemonial [sic] power would be less reluctant (but in some case less obliged) to back its political uses of recognition with supplemental measures."[146]

According to the logic of the Cold War, it is hypothesized that: (1) States belonging to one of the two blocs would grant diplomatic recognition to those belonging to the same bloc. (2) If a state is neutral or non-aligned, it would grant recognition to both sides of a divided nation or neither of them.

It is worth pointing out that the system was not static, even though the bipolarity remained a central feature throughout the period; however, the distribution of power and the level of ideological conflict between the two superpowers changed over time. As the balance of power turned in favor of the Soviet Union, the United States would be less successful in denying diplomatic recognition to the Soviet bloc members, and vice versa.

Meanwhile, when the ideological conflict weakens, bloc members on either side are likely to have more freedom of movement and gain more manoeuvring room to make recognition decisions on their own. As observed by Peterson, "the level of ideological conflict between states is an excellent predictor of the number of expressions of opinion that will be made through recognition decisions."[147]

Therefore, we would expect that: When the level of ideological conflict is high, no cross-bloc recognition is acceptable. It is only with the loosening of tensions

---

144 Jones, 1999: 137.
145 Ringmar, 2002: 115–136.
146 Peterson, 1982: 342.
147 Peterson, 1982: 347.

between the two superpowers that states would grant diplomatic recognition to those political entities on the other side of the curtain.

3.2. Domestic Factors

It is generally agreed that recognition is an acknowledgment of certain facts; hence recognition of a state means to accept its existence as an equal sovereign state in the international system and its government as legitimately in control of its people and area. For instance, Krasner writes that "[t]he basic rule for international legal sovereignty is that recognition is extended to entities, states, with territory and formal juridical autonomy."[148] Gerhard von Glahn and James Larry Taulbee also note that "the basic function of recognition is a formal acknowledgment as *fact* of something that has had uncertain status up to the point of formal acknowledgment."[149]

The emphasis on authority and control over territory and populations also has an important influence on policy makers. In his study of the British and American governments recognition practices, Ti-Chiang Chen summarizes that their official attitude has been "to regard recognition as an acknowledgment of facts, as a declaration that a foreign community had in fact acquired the qualifications of statehood, and as an intimation of willingness to enter into relations with such a community."[150]

There has been a consensus that effective control over all or almost all of the state in question is the necessary condition for recognition. Some scholars and politicians even go so far as to argue that effective control is the sole criterion for recognition. During the Cold War, the effectivist argument became increasingly popular, for instance, the Swiss government found it useful in preserving neutrality, the British government enjoyed its political convenience, and domestic opponents in the United States frequently adopted it in debating over China policy.[151]

As for the divided nations, each of these governments has/had effective control, but the degree varies. Following effectivism, all political entities of divided nations are to be recognized based on what they in fact hold in control.

---

148 Krasner, 1999: 14.
149 Von Glahn and Taulbee, 2017: 200. Italics in original.
150 Chen, 1951: 79.
151 Peterson, 1997: 35–39.

Or it could be argued that when both governments claim to be the sole rightful representative of the entire nation, the one that controls the larger share of territory and/or population seems to stand a better chance.

Nevertheless, Peterson points out that states are not always consistent in their practice, while pursuing an effectivist policy in distant parts of the world, most governments reserved the use of optional criteria to areas closer to home.[152] This brings geography into consideration.

To be sure, geography has always been an important attribute. Only since the Cold War, it becomes more of a fixed issue. Terrified by the upheavals after the First World War and horrified by the devastation of the Second World War, the post-war order is constructed to be "a political-territorial order whose stability was assumed to be the *sine qua non* for global stability."[153] Even though the colonial territories rarely reflected the identity of a pre-existing African socio-political boundary, in most cases, a colony simply transformed into a state with its territorial borders unaffected. Territorial adjustment through warfare is deemed completely illegitimate, the territorial status quo by and large must be preserved. What is more, when dealing with contemporary de facto states and/ or secessionist regions, the underlying framework of the so-called "engagement without recognition" is still the restoration of territorial integrity.[154] Generally speaking, the whole international community tends to guard against the territorial alteration and the creation of new states, which is described by Boaz Arzili as "border fixity."[155] In other words, states are nearly fixed on the map. Therefore, Morgenthau is confident in writing about geography as "[t]he most stable factor upon which the power of a nation depends."[156] In addition, Northedge claims the physical immobility of states to be one of their most important distinguishing features.[157]

Recent quantitative studies confirm geography as an essential factor. Eric Neumayer proclaims that states geographically close to each other are much more likely to enjoy diplomatic exchange.[158] Also, in Timothy Rich's investigation into the diplomatic recognition of Taiwan, distance from Beijing is significant,

---

152 Peterson, 1997: 74.
153 Murphy, 1996: 83.
154 Caspersen, 2018: 373.
155 Atzili, 2012.
156 Morgenthau, 1973: 112.
157 Northedge, 1976: 147–153.
158 Neumayer, 2008: 229.

assuming "that states comparatively distance from the PRC would be more insulated from Beijing's push for recognition."[159]

Therefore, one would expect that a political entity is more likely to receive recognition from states closer to it.

In addition, the domestic system of the political entity also matters. According to Thomas Grant's observation, "democracy began tentatively to emerge as a criterion in the recognition of governments at least as early as it appeared in analyses of the recognition of states."[160] At the heart of this trend lies the influential democratic peace theory, which proposes that the internal makeup of a state will determine its external behavior, and that a democracy is less likely to wage wars. Starting from an empirical fact that democracies hardly ever fight each other, it draws a boundary between peaceful liberal democracies and war-prone non-democracies.[161] Accordingly, non-democracies are threatening both behaviorally and ontologically.[162] Therefore, a new state is more likely to be recognized if it is democratic, for it will be regarded as an expansion of the zone of peace, accelerating the arrival of perpetual peace and benefiting everyone living in the world.

Nonetheless, this is by no means a post-Cold War innovation. Peterson writes that democratic legitimacy began to develop out of British and French willingness to support constitutionalists, in contrast to the Holy Alliance's absolutism.[163] In 1907, five Central American countries – Costa Rica, Guatemala, Honduras, Nicaragua, and Salvador – agreed that they "shall not recognize any other Government which may come into power in any of the five Republics as a consequence of a *coup d'etat*, or of a revolution against the recognized Government, so long as the freely elected representatives of the people thereof have not constitutionally reorganized the country."[164] Edward Carr states that "national self-determination and democracy went hand in hand. Self-determination might indeed be regarded as implicit in the idea of democracy; for if every man's right is recognized to be consulted about the affairs of the political unit to which he belongs, he may be assumed to have an equal right to be consulted about the form and extent of the unit."[165] The American practice since the beginning of

---

159 Rich, 2009: 176.

160 Grant, 1999: 94.

161 Russett, 1994.

162 Hobson, 2008: 75.

163 Peterson, 1997: 58.

164 Papers Relating to the Foreign Relations of the United States, With the Annual Message of the President Transmitted to Congress December 3, 1907, Part II, 1910: 696.

165 Carr, 1947: 39.

the twentieth century demonstrates that "before recognition can be granted," as observed by Northedge, "a foreign political regime must exhibit some of the essential features of a democracy in the Western sense."[166] Shortly after the First World War, Ivor Brown writes about a world "in which every one [sic] is trying to show that he is more democratic than everybody else."[167] It has been rather clear that the central pillar of American foreign policy since Woodrow Wilson is to build a world order comprising only of democratic nation-states.[168] And during the 1950s and 1960s, the Western refused to recognize the GDR on the grounds that it was created without free elections, therefore not in accordance with democratic standards.[169] Additionally, long before the fall of the Berlin Wall, John Dunn has argued that "a democracy is what it is virtuous for a state to be."[170] In a nutshell, since the twentieth century, recognition is considered no longer a means to defend monarchy but a tool to promote democracy.[171]

Recent empirical works also confirm the relevance of the level of democracy in diplomatic practices. According to Bridget Coggins' quantitative analysis on recognition of secessionist movements from 1931 to 2000, great powers have been more likely to grant recognition to foreign secessionists who built a higher level of democracy.[172]

Therefore, it is hypothesized that a political entity that has a higher level of democracy is more likely to be recognized. To be more specific, democracies are more likely to grant recognition to fellow democracies, and might only recognize a political entity after its successful democratization.

3.3. National Identity

Drawing on the social constructivist literature, Wendt defines identity as "relative stable, role-specific understandings and expectations about self."[173] According to him, identities are made, not given, and so are interests. And it is based on identities, that actors define their interests and enter into interactions with each

---

166 Northedge, 1976: 157.
167 Brown, 1920: 175–176.
168 Smith, 1994: 3–4.
169 Crawford, 2006: 456.
170 Dunn, 1979: 11.
171 Dozer, 1966: 322.
172 Coggins, 2014: 74–75.
173 Wendt, 1992: 397.

other. Identities provide answers to these primary questions: Who are we? What distinguishes us from them (others)? What is our role in the world?

Focusing on the relationship between nation and state, Dittmer and Kim argue that national identity is not an attribute of either nation or state, but "the relationship between nation and state that obtains when the people of that nation identify with the state."[174] In this sense, a divided nation is facing a dual crisis of national identity – on the one hand, a sizable segment of the territory and population that would have been included on national grounds is excluded; on the other hand, this same exclusion is defined by both sides as central to the nation's identity. And the division in each of the observed cases coincided with and was reinforced by the Cold War, therefore making it impossible to bridge without some sea change in the international balance of power.[175] They summarize the evolution of national identity as the product of the projected aspirations and demands of the citizenry, the domestic political history, and the foreign policy experience of a nation, which varies over time, reflecting changes inside and outside their boundaries. Nevertheless, the division makes the questions to be answered all the more complicated.

Meanwhile, Sanjoy Banerjee develops a process-tracing model to explain how national identities are formed. National identities are reconstructed as narratives with a certain plot structure, telling of a distinction between the vanguard and laggard elements in the nation, and upholding an achievable destiny and potential dangers for the nation. The story is retold in new situations to provide the logic of its own verification and to provide a guide to action.[176] In the cases of divided nations, national identities are primarily reinterpretations of the past, the present, and the future of the respective nation, articulating a vision that corresponds to the division.

It is important to answer the following questions: Who are we, and whether those who live behind the curtain on the other side are a part of us or not? If yes, then why are we divided? How should we deal with this division? If not, what is the distinction between us and them? Such questions could be expanded further. The answers would affect everyday life of ordinary people living on the border, families and friends unwillingly separated from each other, and undoubtedly be reflected in each part's respective legislation and policies. In Germany, this was called Deutschlandpolitik. In China, it is referred to as Cross-Strait relations.

---

174 Dittmer and Kim, 2018: 13.
175 Dittmer and Kim, 2018: 28–29.
176 Banerjee, 1997: 27–44.

While in Korea and Vietnam, they are simply branded as unification policy. All in all, none of them marks/marked out this field of political-legal action as foreign policy.[177] It is worth pointing out that each of them makes/made similar claims to be the sole representative of the entire nation. Such a claim offers some basic guidance on not only how to deal with the other part, but also how to treat third parties, which, as observed by Gregory Henderson and Richard Ned Lebow, "is designed to buttress one's own identity and legitimacy while weakening that of the other side."[178] Concerning the issue of recognition, the sole representative claim could be read into what the official national identities are, and what the particular government wants to be recognized as.

As claimed by constructivists, recognition is a psychological need. An actor desires to be recognized according to their own self-description. This actor would not sit by passively, in fact, it actively makes its ambition heard and seeks its fulfillment. If not recognized accordingly, it would rather not be recognized at all. This works better to explain, for instance, why Bonn broke up with Belgrade in 1957, and why Beijing has shut itself out of the United Nations for more than two decades.

In general, it is to be expected that when a political entity claims to be more than what it has under effective control, it will be less likely to be recognized.

---

177 For those still suffering under division, none of them treats the other half as foreign. Beijing handles their relations under the Taiwan Affairs Office of the State Council, whose counterpart body is the Mainland Affairs Council directly under the ROC Executive Yuan. On the Korean peninsula, there are the Committee for the Peaceful Reunification of the Fatherland in the North, and the Ministry of Unification in the South.
178 Henderson and Lebow, 1974: 436.

Chapter 4 Quantitative Analysis

Lacking clearly defined criteria, states' recognition practices are extremely complicated, sometimes even controversial. In this study, I will explore potential motivations behind the practice of granting recognition from three different perspectives. First of all, from the international level, the Cold War bipolarity would have a great effect on states' recognition decisions. Secondly, domestic factors could determine an entity's status and popularity in the international community. Last but not least, the entity's self-identity could also be a significant factor.

This chapter focuses on quantitative analysis, starting with the dependent variable and its operationalization. Then I will introduce explanatory variables for diplomatic recognition and their indicators and measurement as well. In the third part I will test these hypotheses and present the results. These rationales and their indicators are not exhaustive; nevertheless, they represent a range of potential motives influencing states' recognition decisions.

4.1. Diplomatic Recognition

The term "diplomatic recognition" refers to the formal acknowledgment and acceptance by State A that B_1 – in the name of either B_1 or B – exists as a state and has an independent government controlling certain territory and representing a certain population. As written in the *Montevideo Convention*, "the recognition of a state may be express or tacit. The latter results from any act which implies the intention of recognizing the new state."[179] It is commonly agreed that recognition may take the form of a congratulatory message to the new-born state on the attainment of independence, or an agreement to establish diplomatic relations. State practice shows that no recognition is implied in the establishment of unofficial representation, various kinds of negotiation, presence at an international conference, the conclusion of a multilateral treaty, or admission to an international organization. As long as State A insists that it does not take steps that amount to recognition, then it does not do so. For example, the United States did not recognize the People's Republic of China until January 1, 1979, even though it accepted the Communists' replacing of the Nationalist representatives in the United Nations in 1971, and Washington and Beijing exchanged liaison offices ever since 1973. As illustrated by the strategy of diplomatic engagement without

---

179 Montevideo Convention, 1933.

recognition, states "can even go so far as to interact with a contested state as though it were recognized in all but name."[180] In short, recognition is a matter of intention. Therefore, one would have to analyze the particular circumstances of each such operation in order to clarify the issue.

It deserves to be noticed that it is not uncommon for states to establish diplomatic relations instead of granting recognition beforehand. In most cases, recognition is a precondition for the establishment of diplomatic relations; however, the absence of diplomatic relations is not equivalent to non-recognition. For instance, the United Kingdom recognized the PRC on January 6, 1950, but they only established diplomatic relations at the level of chargé d'affaires on June 17, 1954, which were then upgraded to the ambassadorial level on March 13, 1972. On the other hand, the non-establishment or withdrawal of diplomatic representation might be a form of non-military sanction, or merely the result of practical considerations. In the instance of US-Cuba relations, the United States cut off its diplomatic ties with the Castro government in 1961 but did not revoke its recognition of the same. No matter how politically hostile to each other, the United States and Cuba did not challenge each other's sovereignty and statehood. In other words, recognition remains in effect despite the termination of bilateral relations. As for states with significantly lesser resources, they are more likely to reduce their diplomatic presences overseas. For example, it would be unreasonable to expect Nauru, a pacific island country with a population of about 10,000, to send diplomats to every foreign capital city. What is more, a large population is not a sufficient condition for sustaining broad overseas presence. Nigeria, the world's seventh largest country by population, announced the closure of four embassies abroad due to budget stringency, as the 2019 budget for diplomatic missions was reported to be only a third of that in 2018, although it is believed to have no impact on its relations with those four states.[181]

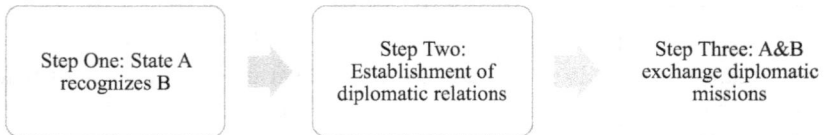

Figure 4-1. Three Steps from Recognition to Exchange of Diplomatic Representations

---

180   Ker-Lindsay, 2015: 285.
181   Campbell, 2019.

When a new state comes into existence, three steps are needed before it can be officially represented in other states' capitals, as shown in Figure 4-1. Recognition is the very first step towards the establishment of diplomatic relations between two states, and the interval between any two steps may differ from case to case. As in the aforementioned UK-PRC case, Step One occurred in 1950, while Step Two and Step Three came four years later. In short, the three steps are distinct but connected: diplomatic representation indicates the existence of diplomatic relations, and diplomatic relations imply state recognition. Therefore, certain steps might be omitted. This pattern is widespread in practice since recognition is a necessary precondition for the establishment of diplomatic relations, and existence of diplomatic relations a prerequisite for the exchange of diplomatic representation.

There are abundant datasets on diplomatic missions exchanged between states. This is quite understandable, since Step Three is the easiest to observe compared to the others. However, as mentioned before, diplomatic exchange is not a synonym for recognition. Therefore, I collect and code my own data based on the official records available, while other secondary sources serve in a consultative manner.

It should be pointed out that there are no distinctions between various patterns of recognition like recognition of state/government and de facto/de jure recognition in the coding process. For our purposes, the recognition of state and government are interchangeable, and there is by no means a meaningful distinction between a de facto and a de jure recognition.[182] To quote Von Glahn and Taulbee, "recognition is recognition."[183]

The dependent variable here is a year-dyadic dichotomous variable, examining the recognition practice of all the system members registered in the Correlates of War project concerning the political entities of divided nations from 1950 to 1990. The COW State System Membership List contains those who are members of the United Nations, or have a population larger than five hundred thousand and host diplomatic missions from two major powers.[184] It should be pointed out that in this research, their self-proclaimed founding dates, instead of the entry dates listed in COW, are adopted – namely the FRG on May 23, 1949, the GDR on October 7, 1949, the PRC on October 1, 1949, the ROC on January 1, 1912,

---

182 For more detailed discussions about different norms and patterns of recognition, see
     Chen, 1951: 97–104, 270–300; Peterson, 1997: 86–100; Shaw, 2017: 329–360.
183 Von Glahn and Taulbee, 2017: 202.
184 Correlates of War, 2017b.

the DPRK on September 9, 1948, the ROK on August 15, 1948, the DRV on
September 2, 1945, and the RVN on October 26, 1955 – because recognition is
generally regarded as retroactive.[185] The dependent variable is set to one if there
is evidence that a state recognizes a political entity of the four divided nations
under consideration in a given year, and zero if not. To enhance the accuracy and
reliability, dates of recognition are sourced directly from the foreign ministries
of individual states and their archives if available, including the German Federal
Foreign Office, PRC Ministry of Foreign Affairs, ROC Ministry of Foreign
Affairs, ROK Ministry of Foreign Affairs, Vietnam Ministry of Foreign Affairs,
and Vietnam National Archives II. When primary source material is unavailable
or inaccessible, secondary sources will also be consulted.

And it is noteworthy that in order to make data suitable for further quantitative analysis, the observation date adopted in this research is December 31,
which means that only the status as of December 31 of the referent year would
be coded. For instance, France and the PRC established diplomatic relations on
January 27, 1964, but the ROC did not break off with France until February 10.
The short period of dual recognition will not be reflected in the data, because on
December 31, 1964, Paris recognized Beijing and only Beijing.

4.2. Explanatory Variables

Although in international law all states are supposed to be equal, in reality the
great powers, by virtue of their extraordinary material capabilities, play an
exceptionally influential role in recognition, and their support would usher in a
cascade of recognition throughout the international system.[186] In Sterio's words,
the great powers "through their recognition practices, often dictate the results of
statehood attempts."[187] And this was especially so in the case of the two superpowers during the Cold War.

Meanwhile, there is a tendency that the great powers prefer coordinated recognition among themselves.[188] Coordination ensures stability. And as observed
by Fabry, "the bigger the disagreements among the powers, the greater the pre-
cariousness of recognition."[189] During the early days of the Cold War, the recognition policies of the United States and the Soviet Union were almost diametrically

---

185 Shaw, 2017: 336.
186 Coggins, 2014: 216–217.
187 Sterio, 2020: 95.
188 Coggins, 2014: 76.
189 Fabry, 2020: 38.

opposed to each other, which made recognition of these entities a dilemma for many other countries. Under these circumstances, the two superpowers made efforts to coordinate their recognition decisions within their own blocs, and then ventured to sell their respective recognition packages to those outside blocs. For convenience, states are categorized in the following analysis according to their relations with the two superpowers,[190] the American allies are categorized as one, the Soviet allies as minus one, and the non-aligned and neutrals as zero.

The balance of power between two superpowers will influence others when choosing sides. As the balance of power between two superpowers changes, so do the recognition decisions of other states. Therefore, it is reasonable to expect that in the case of divided nations the political entity sponsored by a stronger ally tends to be the more attractive. In other words, the stronger the United States, the more likely the FRG, the ROC, the ROK, and the RVN would be recognized by other states; conversely, the stronger the Soviet Union, the more likely the GDR, the PRC, the DPRK, and the DRV would be recognized.

In this research, the realist conception of power is adopted, which implies the ability of states to use material resources to exercise and resist influence on others. And the material capacity is gauged by the widely used Composite Index of National Capacity score from the Correlates of War project. A state's CINC score is a composite calculation of its total population, urban population, iron and steel production, energy consumption, military personnel, and military expenditure, covering the period from 1816 to 2012.[191]

A superpower's material capacity can be measured in both an absolute and a relative manner. To reflect the balance of power between the two superpowers, the relative strength is adopted here, which means using the ratio of a superpower sponsor's CINC score and its superpower rival's score. When the ratio is larger than one, then it is coded a one, indicating that here it will enhance the probability of recognition. In contrast, when the ratio is smaller than one, then it is recorded as a minus one, presuming that this will reduce the probability of recognition. Moreover, when the political entity divorces from its patron, it is supposed that the balance of power between the two superpowers would no longer function as before, hence it is marked a zero.

Furthermore, a dummy variable of whether the year is during the Détente is included to reflect the level of ideological conflict. The Détente began in 1969 as Richard Nixon took office as the President of the United States, and it ended in

---

190 Correlates of War, 2013.
191 Correlates of War, 2017a.

1979, marked by the Soviet invasion of Afghanistan. During this period, the two sides reduced tensions which would make cross-bloc or dual recognition of the divided nations a possible policy option.

Recalling the most frequently quoted criteria listed in the *Montevideo Convention*, a state that merits to be recognized should have a permanent population, a defined territory, government, and the capacity to enter into relations with other states.[192] All the political entities of the four divided nations met these basic qualifications, though their capabilities varied. To gauge their effectiveness and capabilities, two indicators – area and population – are included in this research, using data gathered from the COW National Material Capabilities and Territorial Changes datasets, and official statistics published by individual governments. Generally speaking, larger states are more likely to be active in foreign policy, and also have a higher probability of providing protection and developing a viable economy.[193] In a divided nation, exercising control over a larger population and a larger area seems to make that government a more appropriate representative of the whole nation.

As the political-territorial boundaries stabilized after 1945, states appeared almost fixed on the map; hence geography could also drive foreign policy. In this thesis, the geographical distance is measured as the distance in kilometres between the capital cities of two states, with data taken from the CShapes project – a geographic dataset containing historical maps of state boundaries and capitals from 1946 to 2008.[194] To be sure, plainly measuring the distance between two capital cities might sometimes be misleading. For instance, numerically, Vientiane is located closer to Taipei, 2154 km compared to the 2780km to Beijing. But Laos is adjacent to the People's Republic, and Vientiane consistently has a closer relationship with Beijing. Taking this into account, a small modification is made: If the two entities under observation are bordering each other, then the geographical distance between them is marked as zero; if not, then geographical distance is calculated as the distance between two capital cities, as usual.

The type of domestic political system is also considered to have consequences for the nation-state's behavior on the international stage. And it has been observed that democracies usually do not fight each other, which suggests that to promote democracy is to ensure peace. Therefore, a new state is more likely to be recognized if it is democratic, for it will be regarded as an expansion of the zone of peace, accelerating the arrival of perpetual peace and benefiting

---

192 Montevideo Convention, 1933.
193 Alesina and Spolaore, 2005: 3–4; Hudson and Day, 2020: 170.
194 Weidmann, et al., 2010.

everyone living in the world. As for divided nations, the political entity with a higher level of democracy would be more likely to be recognized.

To gauge the level of democracy, the Polity IV score is adopted in this research.[195] The Polity IV project produces an autocratic-democratic score ranging from -10 (most autocratic) to 10 (most democratic). The project covers almost all the system members listed by the COW except those with a population of less than five hundred thousand. Scores are available from 1800 onward, therefore covering the entire period of this research.

National identities are role-specific understandings and expectations of nation-states, which clearly draw a line between self and others, and also provide the goal to achieve and the guide to act. In divided nations, the official self-descriptions are mainly reflected in the sole representative claims. In China, each of the two regimes on either side of the Taiwan Strait considers itself to be the only rightful government of China. In Germany, the FRG continued to adhere to the Hallstein Doctrine until 1969, while the GDR turned to a two-state-theory as early as 1955. In Korea, the narratives varied: Seoul had its own version of Hallstein Doctrine until 1969. While in the North, up to the armistice at Panmunjom, Pyongyang claimed to be the sole authentic Korean government and attempted to unite the peninsula by force. Having failed to achieve military triumph, Pyongyang tried to solve the problem based on the two-state-theory for the rest of the 1950s, but turned back to the sole representative claim in the 1960s, then it changed tunes again at the beginning of the intra-Korean dialogues. In Vietnam, neither the DRV nor the RVN accepted the other's existence and made every effort to belittle their opponent. In this research, I include a dummy variable for whether the government claims to be the only legitimate representative of the whole nation. This claim is about how it should be, rather than the actual situation; thus, to a certain point, it challenges the principle of effectiveness. Therefore, it is expected that the political entities who make the sole representative claim are less likely to be recognized.

4.3. Hypotheses Tests

In this part, I will use SPSS to conduct a large-N study to test these hypotheses. Before proceeding to the quantitative analysis, all the explanatory variables and respective expected correlations with the diplomatic recognition status are summarized in the following Tables 4-1, 4-2, and 4-3.

---

195 Marshall, et al., 2014.

Table 4-1. Explanatory Variables and Expected Relationships

Variable	Definition	Expectation
BLOC	Whether A and B_i belong to the same bloc or not	Positive
SUPERPOWER	Whether the balance of power between two superpowers is in favor of B_i	Positive
DÉTENTE	Whether the year observed during the Détente	Positive
LN AREA	Territory of B_i	Positive
LN POP	Population of B_i	Positive
LN DISTANCE	Geographical distance between A and B_i	Negative
POLITY	Polity IV score of B_i	Positive
SOLE	Whether B_i claims to be the sole representative	Negative

Table 4-2. Descriptive Analysis

	N	Range	Min.	Max.	Mean		σ
		Statistic	Statistic	Statistic	Statistic	S.E.	Statistic
RECOGNITION	39845	1	0	1	0.520	0.003	0.500
BLOC	39845	1	0	1	0.250	0.002	0.433
SUPERPOWER	39845	2	−1	1	0.012	0.005	0.943
DÉTENTE	39845	1	0	1	0.278	0.002	0.448
LN AREA	39845	5.609	10.468	16.077	12.283	0.008	1.613
LN POP	39513	5.047	8.913	13.960	10.567	0.007	1.345
LN DISTANCE	39845	9.899	0.000	9.899	8.609	0.009	1.742
POLITY	39845	19	−9	10	−4.377	0.032	6.425
SOLE	39845	1	0	1	0.613	0.002	0.487

Table 4-3. Correlation Matrix

	RECOGNITION	BLOC	SUPERPOWER	DÉTENTE	LN AREA	LN POP	LN DISTANCE	POLITY	SOLE
RECOGNITION	1								
BLOC	.265**	1							
SUPERPOWER	.154**	.063**	1						
DÉTENTE	.038**	−.026**	−.025**	1					
LN AREA	.147**	−.224**	−.041**	−0.005	1				
LN POP	.206**	−.160**	−.075**	0.007	.943**	1			
LN DISTANCE	−.101**	−0.004	.013**	−0.004	−.100**	−.096**	1		
POLITY	.244**	.238**	.037**	−.049**	−.030**	.099**	−.107**	1	
SOLE	−.205**	.025**	.110**	−.147**	.247**	.232**	.051**	−.107**	1

**. Significant at 0.01 level (two-tailed).

It is worth noting that the strong correlation between population and territory ($r = 0.943$) might be problematic.

To test the research hypotheses, I employ the binary logistic regression model, which is a predictive model that can be used to forecast the probability of a certain event occurring[196] – diplomatic recognition granted or not. A logistic regression is performed, and the results are reported in Tables 4-4 and 4-5.

Table 4-4. Logistic Regression Model 1: Classification Table

Observed	Predicted		
	No	Yes	% Correct
No	12585	6435	66.2
Yes	4353	16140	78.8
Overall % Correct			72.7

Note: The cut value is 0.500.

---

196 Wilson and Lorenz, 2015: 25–51.

Table 4-5. Logistic Regression Model 1: Variables in the Equation

	B	S.E.	Wald	df	Sig.	Exp(B)
BLOC	1.768	0.032	3067.857	1	0.000	5.859
SUPERPOWER	0.540	0.014	1592.827	1	0.000	1.715
DÉTENTE	0.056	0.026	4.4547	1	0.033	1.058
LN AREA	−0.217	0.025	76.558	1	0.000	0.805
LN POP	0.849	0.030	776.608	1	0.000	2.337
LN DISTANCE	−0.086	0.008	128.960	1	0.000	0.918
POLITY	0.044	0.002	406.996	1	0.000	1.045
SOLE	−1.609	0.028	3305.412	1	0.000	0.200
Constant	−4.771	0.122	1529.087	1	0.000	0.008

Table 4-4 documents the validity of predicted probabilities, which means the model correctly predicted 72.7 % of cases. Table 4-5 shows the contribution of each predictor to the model and their respective statistical significance. In short, all of the predictors are statistically significant ($p < 0.05$). The logistic regression model is best represented as follows:

$$\log\left(\frac{\hat{P}_{\text{RECOGNITION}=1}}{\hat{P}_{\text{RECOGNITION}=0}}\right)$$
$$= -4.771 + 1.768 \text{ BLOC} + 0.540 \text{ SUPERPOWER} + 0.056 \text{ DÉTENTE}$$
$$- 0.217 \text{ LN AREA} + 0.849 \text{ LN POP} - 0.086 \text{ LN DISTANCE}$$
$$+ 0.044 \text{ POLITY} - 1.609 \text{ SOLE}$$

The intercept has a parameter estimate of −4.771, which is when B_1 has no territory, no population, no authority at all. This surely makes no sense here; hence the null hypothesis can be rejected.

Meanwhile, the variable LN AREA reaches the statistically significant level, but against the hypothesized direction, which might be caused by the aforenoted strong population-territory correlation. To figure this out, the regressions are re-performed with each of them respectively marked as Model 1.1 and 1.2. The results are listed in the following Table 4-6.

As illustrated in this table, all the predictors in Model 1.1 and 1.2 are statistically significant, and the directions of correlation are also as expected. Both models have similar accuracy of predictions, 72.6 %; however, comparing their R^2 values, Model 1.1 outperformed Model 1.2. Therefore, it seems better to drop out the variable LN AREA.

Table 4-6. Adjusting Model 1

	Model 1	Model 1.1	Model 1.2
Constant	−4.771**	−4.805**	−4.141**
BLOC	1.768**	1.805**	1.854**
SUPERPOWER	0.540**	0.520**	0.473**
DÉTENTE	0.056**	0.064*	0.096**
LN AREA	−0.217**		0.457**
LN POP	0.849**	0.598**	
LN DISTANCE	−0.086**	−0.080**	−0.075**
POLITY	0.044**	0.051**	0.065**
SOLE	−1.609**	−1.610**	−1.556**
Chi-square	11740.455**	11663.764**	11225.775**
Cox & Snell R Square	0.257	0.256	0.246
Nagelkerke R Square	0.343	0.341	0.327
Overall % Correct	72.7	72.6	72.6

*. Significant at 0.05 level (two-tailed).
**. Significant at 0.01 level (two-tailed).

Taking a closer look at the regression results, the Détente predictor has a p-value higher than the others. Considering that the nominal variable DÉTENTE makes no distinction between the period before and after the Détente, while it would appear that states behave variously during different periods. Therefore, I introduce a categorical variable PERIOD to replace the variable DÉTENTE. The observations made before the Détente are categorized as T1, during the Détente as T2.

Table 4-7. Logistic Regression Model 2: Classification Table

Observed	Predicted		
	No	Yes	% Correct
No	12311	6709	64.7
Yes	4057	16436	80.2
Overall % Correct			72.8

Note: The cut value is 0.500.

Table 4-8. Logistic Regression Model 2: Variables in the Equation

	B	S.E.	Wald	df	Sig.	Exp(B)
BLOC	1.873	0.032	3390.868	1	0.000	6.506
SUPERPOWER	0.495	0.013	1347.628	1	0.000	1.640
LN POP	0.515	0.010	2619.123	1	0.000	1.674
LN DISTANCE	−0.103	0.008	177.595	1	0.000	0.902
POLITY	0.059	0.002	765.362	1	0.000	1.060
SOLE	−1.198	0.030	1583.883	1	0.000	0.302
PERIOD			1470.054	2	0.000	
T1	−1.211	0.032	1466.006	1	0.000	0.298
T2	−0.485	0.030	260.922	1	0.000	0.616
Constant	−3.357	0.130	670.201	1	0.000	0.035

As demonstrated in Table 4-7, the overall correction prediction is 72.8 %, a slight improvement. According to Table 4-8, Model 2 is represented in the following equation:

$$
\log\left(\frac{\hat{P}_{\text{RECOGNITION}=1}}{\hat{P}_{\text{RECOGNITION}=0}}\right)
$$
$$
= -3.357 + 1.873 \text{ BLOC} + 0.495 \text{ SUPERPOWER} + 0.515 \text{ LN POP}
$$
$$
- 0.103 \text{ LN DISTANCE} + 0.059 \text{ POLITY} - 1.198 \text{ SOLE} - 1.211 \text{ T1}
$$
$$
- 0.485 \text{ T2}
$$

In this model, all variables are statistically significant ($p < 0.01$), and the research hypotheses are confirmed.

Also, it should be pointed out that the logistic regression equation presented here is a linear equation, which does not directly predict the outcome of the binary variable RECOGNITION; instead it predicts the log odds that an observation will have an event outcome – diplomatic recognition in this case.

Now let us try to explain why State A recognized B_i with the above quantitative analyses results. So far, it could be interpreted that the Cold War logic was dominant, as states from the same bloc were above six times more likely to grant one another diplomatic recognition. Tipping the balance between the two superpowers towards its sponsor was also associated with an increase in that entity's possibility of obtaining recognition. Before the Détente, states generally refrained from choosing sides between divided nations; therefore, if the observation was made before 1969, the entity B_i was about three times less likely to obtain diplomatic recognition.

As for national attributes, it could be concluded that those political entities with a larger size were more likely to be recognized. Moreover, all political entities were usually more likely to be recognized by neighboring states, than those far away. Meanwhile, states with a higher level of democracy would have a slightly better chance to obtain diplomatic recognition.

Furthermore, if B_1 was devoted to the sole representative claim and insisted on being recognized as B, it would be roughly three times more likely to be denied such a diplomatic recognition.

4.4. Conclusion

Why could B_1 – a political entity of a divided nation, whose legitimacy has been constantly challenged by a rivaling B_2 – manage to win diplomatic recognition from State A? All our candidates are qualified as a state in the sense that each of them has a permanent population, a defined territory, its own government, and the capacity to enter into relations with other states – the four elements defined in the *Montevideo Convention*. The ideologically divided world made sure that they were recognized by certain members of the system, while denied recognition by those on the opposite side. The empirical research presented here confirms the expectation that the two superpowers played influential roles in the recognition decisions of others. Standing in the same bloc would usually lead to mutual recognition. Nevertheless, states might also switch their allegiance to the other side. In other words, bipolarity was dominant but it did not preclude the possibility of cross-bloc recognition. When the balance of power between the two superpowers changes, it is more likely for states to make or change their recognition decisions.

The traditional effectivist principle remains significant. Generally speaking, B_i with a larger size turned out to have a greater probability of receiving diplomatic recognition.

Although geography is an important consideration in political decisions, when facing two rival state candidates, the geographic effect could be easily counterweighed for the fact that the close the geographical distance between State A and B_1 could always mean that the geographical distance between A and B_2 is not much greater. Therefore, it is quite acceptable that there is only a marginal increase observed in the likelihood of diplomatic recognition occurring between those pairs that are geographically closer to each other.

It could be concluded that states are more likely to grant diplomatic recognition to those political entities that have a slightly higher level of democracy. The correlation seems not strong enough to claim that recognition functioned as the promoter for liberal internationalism.

Besides, the quantitative analysis highlighted the importance of national identity. When a part of the divided nation identified itself as the only rightful representative of the entire nation, it was seeking recognition based on the normative value of national integrity instead of the substantial facts. If the entity stuck to the sole representative claim, it would see a reduction in the likelihood of its diplomatic recognition.

In sum, all of the research hypotheses received significant support. But correlation does not necessarily lead to causation, as correlational analysis excludes the exploration of mechanism. In the next chapter, I will try to uncover the dynamics involved through comparative case analysis.

Chapter 5 Comparative Study

"To be known. To be heard. To have one's unique identity recognized and seen as worthy. It was a universal human desire, I thought, as true for nations and peoples as it was for individuals."[197]

Barack Obama

The Cold War had its origins in two processes that took place around the turn of the twentieth century – one is the rise of the United States and the Soviet Union as two supercharged empires, and the other is the ever-sharpening ideological division between capitalism and its critics.[198] The two superpowers split the world into their own spheres of influence, and the divided nations undoubtedly marked the front line of the Cold War. Some of them suffered from bloody military confrontation, some not, but all of them were caught in the struggle for recognition.

5.1. China

The Unfinished Civil War

As a victor in the Second World War, China under the leadership of Jiang Jieshi recovered its territory from Japanese militarism and colonialism, including not only a large part of mainland China but also Taiwan and the surrounding islands. However, the surrender of Japan did not ensure peace. The civil war reignited in 1946. Back to that time, the CCP had only 1.2 million poorly equipped armed forces in the "liberated areas," while the KMT commanded far better equipped troops of 4.3 million and enjoyed broad international support, in control of three-quarters of the country with three-quarters of the population.[199] The KMT gained an early and quick advantage until the CCP completely turned the tide on the battlefield in 1948. After three decisive campaigns in this year, the future of Nationalist regime was doomed, and the capital city Nanjing was abandoned once again. On January 19, 1949, the Foreign Ministry telegraphed

---

197 Obama, 2020: 448.
198 Westad, 2017.
199 Li, 2018: 53.

all foreign embassies to move to Guangzhou.[200] On January 21, Jiang was forced to resign from his presidency. On August 5, the Truman administration released its White Paper defending its China policy against the blame for losing China, which left the impression that the United States was washing its hands, while the Nationalist forces were still fighting the Communists in the south. Moreover, the Chinese Communists were portrayed as Soviet puppets in the China White Paper, which irritated the Communists and further fueled the already fervent anti-American sentiment in China.[201] Mao Zedong wrote several articles for Xinhua News Agency criticizing the White Paper as "a counter-revolutionary document which openly demonstrates U.S. imperialist intervention in China."[202] He went on further and interpreted the White Paper as a confession that "the great, sanguinary war of the last few years, which cost the lives of millions of Chinese, was planned and organized by U.S. imperialism."[203]

On October 1, 1949, Mao Zedong proclaimed the establishment of the People's Republic of China in Beijing. The new regime was immediately recognized by the Soviet bloc countries, and then several Asian neighbors, though it took several months to take some southern provinces under control.

The Republic of China's central government finally relocated to Taipei on December 7, 1949, with 600,000 armed forces and about 2 million KMT-sympathizers retreated to Taiwan. Although some forty states maintained diplomatic relations with ROC, only three of them had missions in Taipei, namely South Korea, the United States, and the Philippines.[204] There have been continued debates over the status between the Taiwan Strait; nonetheless, the war had never been formally ended between the two sides even until the present day.

---

200 The government was pulled out of Nanjing in April, Guandong in October, and Chongqing in December. But most countries diplomats did not follow this retreat. Klein, 1963: 45.
201 Rintz, 2009: 76–84.
202 Mao, 1961: 442.
203 Mao, 1961: 451.
204 Chou, 2001: 3.

Table 5-1. Diplomatic Recognition of the PRC/ROC by the end of 1949

PRC	ROC		
Albania	Afghanistan	Ecuador	Peru
Bulgaria	Argentina	Egypt	Philippines
Burma	Australia	Finland	Portugal
Czechoslovakia	Bahamas	France	Saudi Arabia
Germany, DR	Belgium	Greece	Korea, R
Hungary	Bolivia	Iran	Sweden
India	Brazil	Iraq	Switzerland
Korea, DPR	Canada	Italy	South Africa
Mongolia	Ceylon	Luxembourg	Thailand
Poland	Chile	Mexico	Turkey
Romania	Colombia	Netherlands	United Kingdom
Soviet Union	Costa Rica	New Zealand	United States
	Cuba	Norway	Uruguay
	Denmark	Nicaragua	Venezuela
	Dominica	Panama	

To put it bluntly, the mainland China has a land some 270 times greater than that of the island Taiwan, and the PRC has a population 60–70 times larger than that of Taiwan, as illustrated in Figure 5-1. The huge difference provides a convincing evidence that the PRC is the real China.

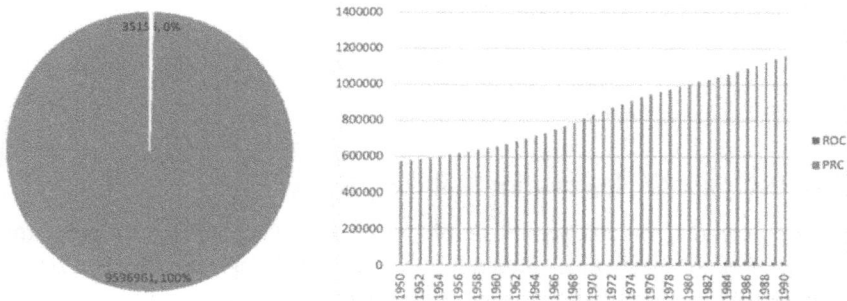

Figure 5-1. China: Area and Population

Several Western countries swiftly accept the situation. Subsequently, the United Kingdom recognized the People's Republic on January 6, 1950, followed by Denmark (January 9), Finland (January 13), Sweden (January 14), Switzerland (January 17), and the Netherlands (March 27).

At the onset of 1950, the Taiwan Strait seemed not broad enough to save the Nationalists from the final cracking down.[205] Moreover, Secretary of State Dean Acheson made a speech on January 12, 1950 that placed Taiwan out of the US defense perimeter. It was widely believed that the United States was prepared to recognize the Communist China.[206] The effectivist principle prevailed.

It should be pointed out that no one proposed to use the political system as the criteria or a precondition for recognition. For the Chinese Communists, any precondition is unacceptable. This point has been made clear by Mao Zedong in his discussions on diplomacy ahead of the founding of the PRC.[207] On the other side, the system under Jiang's rule could not be labeled as a democratic one by any means, as shown in Figure 5-2.

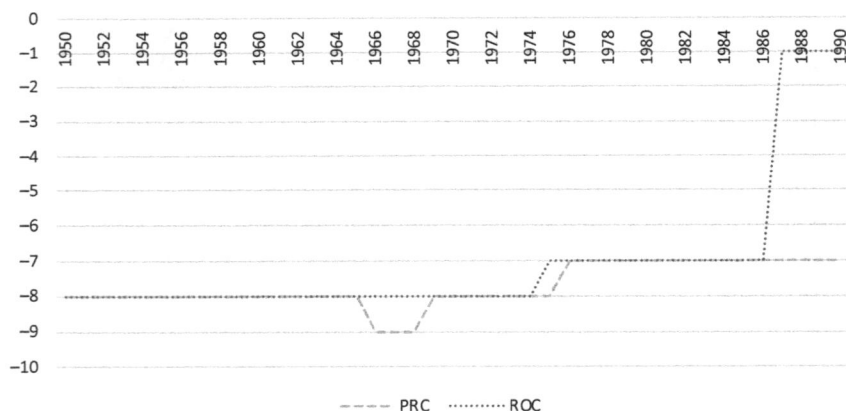

Figure 5-2. China: Polity Scores

The PRC onto the International Stage

In the very first official statement of the Central People's Government, the People's Republic of China claimed itself to be the sole legal government representing all of the Chinese people and expressed its willingness "to establish diplomatic relations with any and all governments of foreign countries which wish to observe principles of equality, mutual benefit, and mutual respect for territorial

---

205 Finkelstein, 1993: 198; Li, 2018: 70–71.
206 Thayer, 1974: 107.
207 Mao, 1961: 405–408, 411–423.

sovereignty."[208] As the Foreign Minister, Zhou Enlai sent Mao's proclamation by letter to all the former consular offices of various countries in Beijing, requesting them to forward it to their governments. In this letter, he also affirmed that "it is necessary to establish normal diplomatic relations between the People's Republic of China and all countries of the world."[209]

The Soviet Union responded immediately on October 2 by terminating the relations with Yan Xishan government in Guandong, considering that the Yan Xishan government had ceased exercising authority in the country, turned into Provincial Government of Guandong and lost the possibility of maintaining diplomatic relations with foreign governments in the name of China.[210] Through exchanging telegrams between Andrei Gromyko, the Deputy Minister for Foreign Affairs, and Zhou, the Soviet Union became the very first state to recognize the PRC, and they decided to establish diplomatic relations and exchange ambassadors right away. The other socialist states followed suit.

As already announced before the founding of the PRC, Mao's foreign policy was "Leaning to One Side," namely to join the socialist camp in the post-war world. As in his *On the People's Democratic Dictatorship*, Mao argued that "all Chinese without exception must lean either to the side of imperialism or to the side of socialism. Sitting on the fence will not do, nor is there a third road. We oppose the Chiang Kai-shek [Jiang Jieshi] reactionaries who lean to the side of imperialism, and we also oppose the illusions about a third road."[211] From December 1949 to February 1950, Mao visited Moscow and discussed the division of labor with Stalin. As a result, China was formally carved into the Cold War as the sign of the Sino-Soviet Treaty of Friendship, Alliance, and Mutual Assistance on February 14, 1950. Historians agreed that the alliance between Beijing and Moscow was "the cornerstone of the global communist alliance system in the Cold War."[212]

In the meantime, neighboring Asian states watched the situation in China with cautions and concerns. On December 16, 1949, Burma recognized the PRC, which was not only the first Asian but also the first non-Communist country to do so. India was the most strident one in recognizing the new regime: it recognized the PRC on December 30, 1949, and the diplomatic relations were

---

208 Archives of the Ministry of Foreign Affairs, 2006b: 9.
209 Archives of the Ministry of Foreign Affairs, 2006b: 10.
210 Archives of the Ministry of Foreign Affairs, 2006b: 16.
211 Mao, 1961: 415.
212 Li, 2018: 64.

formally established on April 1, 1950. Jawaharlal Nehru viewed the Communist victory as a boost to nationalism and firmly supported the PRC's admission to the United Nations. Indonesia too recognized the PRC quickly. Moreover, it was believed that the Philippines was also inclined to recognize the new regime.[213] In the Middle East, Israel was the first to make the decision to recognize the PRC. However, reluctant to irritate the Arab world, Beijing turned a deaf ear. And Israel, on the other side, afraid of challenging Washington, made no further attempts to establish relations with Beijing.[214]

The PRC also attempted to undercut the ROC's international status. In November 1949, Zhou Enlai sent Secretary-General Trygve Lie an official communication, informing the formation of the PRC and demanding the expulsion of the ROC from the United Nations.[215] However, the Soviet-sponsored resolution calling for the expulsion of the ROC failed during the Security Council meetings in January 1950. It is noteworthy that at that time it was universally accepted that the question of Chinese representation was a procedural matter and could be decided by a simple majority without a veto.[216] As a protest to the presence of ROC representative, the Soviet representative walked out of the Security Council, which turned out to place the Soviet bloc at a tactical disadvantage when the war broke out in Korea. In the early months of 1950, the efficacy of the United Nations was seriously challenged, as Lie complained that "the UN's stock was at its lowest ebb as a result of the dispute over recognition of a Chinese Government."[217]

As the Korean War broke out on June 25, 1950, Washington gave a second thought on Taiwan's strategic position. President Truman ordered the Seventh Fleet to the Taiwan Strait to prevent any attack on the island and called upon the KMT forces to stop all air and sea operations against the mainland.[218] Regardless of strong protest from Beijing, this American intervention did not attract much attention worldwide while there was an ongoing war fighting on the Korean peninsula. Moreover, the conflict further escalated in October as Mao sent the

---

213 Colbert, 1977: 133–134.
214 Sufott, 2007: 94–96.
215 Zhou, 1949.
216 Luard, 1971: 730. At that time, the composition of the Security Council was China, Cuba, Ecuador, Egypt, France, India, Norway, the Soviet Union, the United Kingdom, the United States, and Yugoslavia. Five of them recognized the PRC, but in minimum seven votes were needed to seat the Chinese Communists.
217 Goodwin, et al., 1976: 200.
218 United States. Department of State, 1950: 5.

Chinese People's Volunteer Army to rescue the North Korean regime. Despite repeated warnings about potential Chinese military intervention, the Americans not only failed to prepare for this intervention, but also refused to believe that Beijing could operate independently of Moscow.[219] Although both sides refrained from triggering a third world war, the Korean War, which started as a civil war between North and South Korea, now became a conflict between the new China and the United States, with each side depicting the other in the darkest colors. As a result, the relations between Washington and Beijing could not be worse.

During the Korean War, the PRC has not scored any more on the diplomatic front, with the only exception of establishing relations with the adjacent Pakistan on May 21, 1951.

The Korean War was celebrated as a great victory for the Chinese had rolled back the world's most powerful forces. After a hundred years of humiliation, no doubt it could boost the legitimacy of the new regime in China. On the other hand, the Korean War brought the new China enormous challenges from all aspects.[220] One of the consequences is that Beijing had to postpone indefinitely the scheduled operation to liberate Taiwan, so the KMT survived on the island.[221]

After the armistice in Korea, the Chinese Communist leadership found two major tasks: preparing for the First Five Year Plan at home and reducing hostilities from abroad.[222] The PRC advocated peaceful coexistence in diplomacy to win international sympathy and support for the new regime on the one hand, and to drive a wedge between the United States and its main allies on the other.

The Geneva Conference of 1954, aiming at ending the hostilities in both Korea and Indochina, provided the People's Republic with a valuable opportunity for the first time to sit together with the great powers and appear in an important international meeting. The CCP assigned two goals to the Chinese delegation: first, to engage in active diplomacy to break the American isolation and embargo towards China, and to ease tensions globally; and second, to conclude agreements, thus paving the way for solving international conflicts through negotiations among great powers.[223]

---

219 Li, 2018: 81.
220 For detailed discussions on China's gains and losses in fighting the Korean War, See Chen, 1997: 220–222; Shen, 2004: 448–451; Yang, 2009: 142–143.
221 Yang, 2009: 107.
222 Zhang, 2007: 510.
223 Wang, 1985: 5–6.

During the conference, the Chinese and the western powers interacted frequently. Sino-British relations made a breakthrough with the establishment of diplomatic relations at the level of chargé d'affaires on June 17.[224] Meanwhile, with close consultation and cooperation among Chinese, Soviets, and Vietnamese, they reached a moderate agreement with France that brought an end to the First Indochina War. In spite of American opposition and delaying tactics, the Geneva Conference turned out to be a diplomatic triumph for Beijing. The *People's Daily* published an editorial on July 22, 1954, which expressed the boosting pride and confidence of the Chinese Communists: "For the first time as one of the Big Powers, the People's Republic of China joined the other major powers in negotiations on vital international problems and made a contribution of its own that won the acclaim of wide sections of world opinion. The international status of the People's Republic of China as one of the big world powers has gained universal recognition. Its international prestige has been greatly enhanced. The Chinese people take the greatest joy and pride in the efforts and achievements of their delegation at Geneva."[225]

In its diplomatic debut, the PRC adopted a moderate tone and changed its belligerent image. Zhou Enlai and his delegation impressed the world with their shrewd and flexibility. "Showing willingness to play an active, flexible, responsible and conciliatory role in resolving international disputes," as commented by Shu Guang Zhang, "the regime wished to be recognized as a 'normal' and major power in the Cold War politics."[226] Such a development was by and large welcomed. Later this year, Norway and the Netherlands established diplomatic relations with the PRC, respectively.

It should not be ignored that when the Geneva Conference broke for a recess, Zhou Enlai swiftly departed for New Delhi and Rangoon, where he met Jawaharlal Nehru and U Nu, respectively. On June 28, Zhou and Nehru issued a joint statement declaring the Five Principles of Peaceful Coexistence as the framework for their relations with all other countries and the best solution to the Indochina problem.[227] U Nu and Zhou also enunciated the Five Principles as

---

224 Because of London's continuing support of ROC's representative in the United Nations, Beijing rejected the complete normalization of Sino-British relations. This model also applied to the Netherlands later. For a detailed record on the establishment of Sino-British relations, see Archives of the Ministry of Foreign Affairs, 2006a: 402–431. For a discuss on this tactic, see also Mao, 1998: 167.
225 *People's Daily*, July 22, 1954, 1.
226 Zhang, 2007: 518.
227 The Five Principles of Peaceful Coexistence, also known as Panchsheel: (1) Mutual respect for each other's territorial integrity and sovereignty; (2) Mutual non-aggression;

principles guiding the relations between Burma and China.[228] The Five Principles of Peaceful Coexistence were not an empty declaration but a shrewd response "to the perceived effort by the contending American and Soviet superpowers to subordinate smaller states and incorporate them into their competing spheres of influence."[229]

This is the milestone as the PRC oriented itself to the Third World. With the support of India and Burma, Zhou Enlai made China's peaceful intentions known among its Asian neighbors, thus paving the way to Bandung.

The Bandung Conference, also known as Asian-African Conference, was the first large-scale meeting of Asian and African states, which took place on April 18–24, 1955, in Bandung. Initiated by Burma, Ceylon, India, Indonesia, and Pakistan, this conference aimed at opposing colonialism, and promoting economic, cultural, and political cooperation between Afro-Asian states.[230] Altogether twenty-nine Asian and African states participated in it, and most of them are newly independent nations. The Bandung Conference provided both opportunities and challenges to the PRC. Of all the twenty-nine countries, twenty-two had no diplomatic relations with Beijing, and many of them maintained official relations with Taipei. The majority of them remained suspicious, even hostile toward the PRC.[231]

Fortunately surviving an assassination attempt on his way to Bandung, Zhou Enlai, showing his personal charisma and diplomatic skills, played an important role in the conference. In his famous speech delivered on April 19, Zhou carefully avoided using ideological languages, and emphasized the common suffering and experience: "The Chinese Delegation has come here to seek common ground, not to create divergence. Is there any basis for seeking common ground among us? Yes, there is. The overwhelming majority of the Asian and African countries and peoples have suffered and are still suffering from the calamities of colonialism. This is acknowledged by all of us. If we seek common ground in doing away with the sufferings and calamities under colonialism, it will be very easy

---

(3) Mutual non-interference in each other's internal affairs; (4) Equality and mutual benefit; and (5) Peaceful co-existence. Zhong gong zhong yang wen xian yan jiu shi, 1997: 426–428.

228 Zhong gong zhong yang wen xian yan jiu shi, 1997: 429.
229 Freeman, 2020: 42.
230 Archives of the Ministry of Foreign Affairs, 2007: 18–19.
231 Zhang, 2007: 522.

for us to have mutual understanding and respect, mutual sympathy and support, instead of mutual suspicion and fear, mutual exclusion and antagonism..."[232]

In concern of the precarious situation in the Taiwan Straits, which might precipitate a Sino-American military confrontation and escalate into a third world war in many delegates' viewpoint, Zhou issued a press statement declaring that "the Chinese Government is willing to sit down and enter into negotiations with the United States Government to discuss the question of relaxing tension in the Far East and especially the question of relaxing tension in the Taiwan area."[233]

By adopting a rather surprisingly conciliatory stance, Zhou calmed fears of some anti-communist delegates and reconciled and/or strengthened China's relations with other nations. Meeting privately with leaders from neighboring countries, Zhou reiterated that China had no aggressive ambitions, and it would not attempt to export revolution.[234] To reassure the royal government in Laos and Cambodia, Zhou also arranged meetings with the DRV delegation, where Pham Van Dong promised to respect the sovereignty of both countries.[235] Moreover, Zhou signed the Dual Nationality Treaty with Indonesia, which alleviated the shaky newly independent state's concerns about using overseas Chinese as a potential fifth column.[236] The Thai and Philippine governments also welcomed such a step.[237] Gamal Abdel Nasser was under concentrated diplomatic offensive, which not only led to Egypt's recognition of the PRC, but also opened a door to the Arab world and the African continent.[238]

As Homer Alexander Jack pointed out in 1955, "Bandung saw the emergence of China as a great Asian power and not merely as an isolated partner of Russia."[239] Put differently, since Bandung, the Communist leaders consciously identified and depicted their new China to be a part of the Third World, striving for independence and sovereignty, with neither intention nor capability of aggression.[240] In short, Bandung marked the watershed of Chinese diplomacy.[241]

In the following decade after Bandung, the world witnessed a rapid decolonializing process. Perceiving decolonization as a part of the struggle against

232 Poplai, 1955: 21.
233 Kahin, 1956: 28–29; Archives of the Ministry of Foreign Affairs, 2007: 75.
234 Zhong gong zhong yang wen xian yan jiu shi, 1997: 511–515.
235 Colbert, 1977: 326.
236 Mackie, 2010: 9–26.
237 Zhang, 2007: 524.
238 Mao, 2010: 89–108.
239 Jack, 1955: 36.
240 Zhang, 2007: 525.
241 Shinn and Eisenman, 2012: 33; Niu, 2013: 502.

imperialists, Beijing actively supported the African nations, both rhetori-
cally and materially. For instance, Beijing promptly backed Nasser during the
Suez Crisis and aided the National Liberation Front in the Algerian War.[242]
Zhou Enlai's ten-country visit at the end of 1963 and beginning of 1964 was
the most dramatic. Zhou unveiled the principles guiding China-Africa relations, and presented eight principles for aid policy with a particular emphasis
on self-reliance, which continued to be widely quoted or echoed by Chinese
officials to the present.[243] China's aid to Africa grew significantly after Zhou's
tour.[244]

The PRC identified itself as a socialist developing country belonging to the
Third World. As the Sino-Soviet relations worsened, Beijing strived to form a
Third World united front against the two superpowers at the same time.[245] Put
in Maoist phrase, this was a strategy to unite the Third World against the First
World.[246] In hindsight, this strategy did not work as envisioned by the CCP leaders. Nevertheless, the Third World solidarity had been at the heart of China's
diplomacy ever since then, which proved to be more reliable and enduring than
the alliance between Communist comrades.[247] It has been argued that the iden-
tification with the Third World has been one of the most consistent themes in
Beijing's foreign policy pronouncements.[248]

Beijing's strident support for the national liberation movement boosted its
prestige in the Third World; however, it unavoidably alienated itself from former
colonial masters in West Europe. For instance, it was believed that France was
considering recognizing the PRC as early as 1949, but such a decision was postponed due to Beijing's role in Vietnam and Algeria.[249] Until January 1964, their
shared nuclear isolation and agreement on American withdrawal from Vietnam
finally brought Beijing and Paris together, albeit the Sino-French rapprochement
did not trigger a chain effect toward universal recognition nor break the dam for

---

242 Larkin, 1973: 24–28.
243 Larkin, 1973: 65–70; Brazinsky, 2017: 347–348.
244 Jiang, 2016: 102.
245 Yu, 1977: 1039.
246 According to Mao, the United States and the Soviet Union belong to the First World,
     the Second World comprises Europe, Japan, Australia, Canada and other capitalist
     countries, while the Third World comprises Asia, Africa and Latin America. Mao,
     1998: 545.
247 Niu, 2013: 503.
248 Van Ness, 2018: 194–214.
249 Zhai, 2012: 14–17.

its entry into the United Nations as expected.[250] Under the American pressure, Japan, Canada, and other European capitalist countries had to uphold Taipei's One China. By and large, the Cold War logic remained prevalent during the 1960s. Nonetheless, the CCP leaders were confident that the Chinese market was attractive to all the profit-driving capitalist countries, and it was impossible to ignore the political importance of Beijing. Therefore, sooner or later, they would accord recognition to the PRC.

In short, the decade after Bandung witnessed the PRC coming out from the diplomatic isolation. The number of states that had diplomatic relations with Beijing almost doubled in this decade, from twenty-seven in 1955 to fifty-three in 1965. It was also in 1965 that Beijing first caught up the votes in the United Nations.[251] Undeniably, Beijing's international status rose significantly.

This trend was interrupted by the Chinese Communists themselves. The Cultural Revolution caused problems at home and abroad as Beijing's policy radicalized. In 1966, Beijing recalled all its ambassadors back home, except Huang Hua in Cairo. During the chaotic period, the PRC's progress in diplomatic recognition was slow down.[252] Beijing sank into isolation as a result of its anti-imperialist and anti-revisionist revolutionary diplomacy. To make matters worse, the Sino-Soviet ideological dispute degenerated into military confrontation along the border.[253] Nevertheless, Beijing's aid continued as a means to achieve Third World unity. The most extraordinary project was the Tanzania-Zambia railway, a commitment made in 1967 and completed in 1975.[254]

After the Party Congress in April 1969, the CCP leaders reevaluated the international situation. The Soviet Union replaced the United States as the No.1 enemy of China, and the American card should be played.[255] To avoid a two-front war, Beijing once again turned to a more moderate foreign policy, actively seeking to improve relations with other countries. The return to normalcy, coinciding with the Détente, led to the recognition from a bunch of countries all over the world, the replacement of the China's seat in the United Nations in 1971, Nixon's historic trip to China in 1972, and eventually the normalization of relations between Beijing and Washington in 1979. It is worth noting that it took

---

250 Lüthi, 2014: 111–145.
251 Gao, 1993: 190.
252 Friedman, 2015: 150–155.
253 Lüthi, 2008: 341–344.
254 Xinhua News Agency, 1989: 376–377.
255 Li and Xia, 2018: 252.

nearly a decade from US-PRC rapprochement to formal diplomatic recognition, the major reason was Beijing's insistence of One China.

For sure, the 1970s witnessed the great change of the PRC, both in its leadership and its policies. Both Mao and Zhou passed away in 1976. After a short period of transition, Deng Xiaoping became the predominant leader in 1978. Their experiences and personalities varied, but they shared the beliefs in values of national sovereignty and territorial integrity. They insisted that Taiwan is an inalienable part of China which should be reunited with the mainland.[256] Since Deng's time, Beijing gradually adopted a more benign tone, dropped the slogan of "liberation of Taiwan," and proposed to achieve national unification under the framework of One Country, Two Systems.[257]

From then on, the PRC became an active player within the international system, while no one would seriously challenge its position as the sole representative of China for any longer.

The ROC Survived

In a way, the outbreak of the Korean War resembled the Japanese attack on Pearl Harbor, both of which led to an alliance between the United States and the Republic of China – this time, "a second marriage of convenience."[258] As the hostility between Washington and Beijing grew, the bond between Washington and Taipei strengthened. As a corollary to the Korean War, Taipei gained not only "an unequalled opportunity to survive the risk of imminent attack" but also "a brighter outlook for its diplomacy."[259]

The massive influx of military supplies and economic assistance to the island was in stark contrast to the halfhearted aid during the civil war. In fact, the ROC was the largest recipient of American economic aid per capita before it finally graduated in the 1960s.[260] This time, the KMT learned lessons from its debacle on the mainland and made good use of the American aid in pursuit of stability on the island.[261]

---

256 Zhang, 2014: 908–909.
257 Deng, 1993: 30–31; 34–36. Its main target is Taiwan, but this policy was first applied in Hong Kong, and Macau.
258 Kirby, 2001: 45.
259 Chou, 2001: 5.
260 Taylor, 2009: 484.
261 Kirby, 2001: 41–44.

As the climax of the American commitment, the United States and the Republic of China signed the Mutual Defense Treaty on December 2, 1954 which formally made Taiwan a part of the American security system. While protecting Taiwan and Penghu from Communist attack, the United States ruled out any unilateral Nationalist military offensive action to retake the mainland.[262] The KMT paid the price for the new alliance, for the treaty shattered any real hope of military recovery of the mainland. Nevertheless, Jiang viewed the treaty as his greatest diplomatic success after the defeat in the mainland that secured his power base in Taiwan and demonstrated American determination to continue recognition of Taipei.[263]

In general, Jiang's foreign policy can be summarized as: (1) consolidate the ROC's legitimate status in the United Nations, and prevent the entry of the PRC; (2) improve the relations with the United States, seek American military and economic assistance; (3) urge the democratic free nations with whom the ROC had diplomatic relations to send envoys to Taiwan to set up diplomatic missions to maintain and enhance mutual friendship, and prevent them from recognizing the PRC; (4) strengthen mutual assistance with Asian anti-communist countries to form the Far East Anti-Communist Front; (5) restore diplomatic relations with defeated countries, Japan and Germany, and establish friendly relations; (6) support the national independence movement, strive for friendship with newly independent states, and quickly establish diplomatic relations with them; (7) as for those neutral states have no relations with neither the PRC nor the ROC, positively try to establish diplomatic relations with them, or prevent them from recognizing the PRC on the negative side; (8) as for democratic states that have recognized the PRC, keep in touch with them directly or indirectly, urge them to help to oppose the PRC, and take the position in ROC's favor in the Cold War; (9) sever diplomatic relations with those who recognize the PRC, to defy the conspiracy to create the so-called "two Chinas"; and (10) strengthen trade relations, cultural exchanges, technical cooperation, and mutual visits with Free World countries to enhance mutual friendship.[264]

The seat in the United Nations, especially in the Security Council remained high in Jiang's priority. In the meantime, the Americans were determined to keep the Nationalists seated on the Security Council as the representative of China. On February 1, 1951, the General Assembly adopted a resolution condemning

---

262 United Nations, 1956: 213–225.
263 Lin, 2013: 971–994.
264 Gao, 1993: 28.

the PRC as an aggressor in Korea, which was used by the Americans as an argument to keep the PRC out of the United Nations.[265] During the 1950s, the United States successfully mobilized a great majority to exclude the Soviet proposal to seat the PRC from the agenda of the United Nations General Assembly.[266]

The voting pattern began to change as after 1955 more and more states were admitted into the United Nations, see the following Table 5-2. In ending the "logjam," the organization and its members laid down the principle of universality.[267] The exclusion of the authority that controlled the largest population in the world was undoubtedly in defiance of the principle of universal membership. These newcomers, especially the newly independent countries, gradually challenged Taipei's claim to be the legal representative of China in the United Nations. Alarmed by this trend and the growing Bandung spirit as well, Taipei adopted a more active diplomacy, which turned to be rather successful in Middle East and Latin America.[268]

Table 5-2. Voting Records on Chinese Representation in the United Nations

	For	Against	Abstention
1951	11	37	4
1952	7	42	11
1953	10	44	2
1954	11	43	6
1955	12	42	6
1956	24	47	8
1957	27	47	7
1958	28	44	9
1959	29	44	9
1960	34	42	22

Facing the changing political complexion of the United Nations, a new strategy was developed in 1961 to prevent the expulsion of the ROC. The United States, along with Australia, Colombia, Italy, and Japan, introduced a draft resolution to characterize the question of the representation of China as an "important question," thus requiring a two-thirds majority for a dispositive decision.[269]

---

265 United Nations General Assembly, 1951; Goodwin, et al., 1979: 224.
266 Yang, 1997: 186–190.
267 Grant, 2009: 63–67.
268 Klein, 1963: 46.
269 United Nations General Assembly, 1961b.

Taipei held an upper hand in the diplomatic competition due to the long existence of the ROC. However, the scenario was quite different in Africa. In any event, there were only three independent states – Ethiopia, Liberia, and South Africa – and a semi-independent Egypt before the KMT was defeated in the mainland. As illustrated in Table 5-1, the ROC-Africa relations were marginal at best. The ROC leaders only developed a political interest as a result of the fierce competition with the PRC to be the sole representative of China.[270] Taipei only established diplomatic relations with Liberia in 1957. Anticipating the decolonization of Africa, Taipei launched a series of diplomatic offensives to secure recognition from those newly independent states. Since December 1959, several ROC goodwill missions visited eleven new-born states and two about-to-be states.[271] As a result, the ROC established diplomatic relations with eight states, half of those who gained independence in 1960.[272] The momentum of the ROC-African relations was Foreign Minister Shen Changhuan's sixteen states visit in July to August 1963. By the end of the year, nineteen of the thirty-three independent African states had diplomatic relations with Taipei.[273]

The ROC's major instrument in Africa was agricultural aid. Taking geographic and economic factors into consideration, the ROC judged that it could win friendship from Africa by providing technical assistance on agriculture. The project was enthusiastically endorsed by the United States, who actually provided financial support for it.[274] In January 1961, the ROC launched the Operation Vanguard, with ROC's Mr. Africa Yang Xikun as the coordinator responsible for its implementation. In October, the ROC sent its first agricultural mission to Liberia. Shen's visit in 1963 also brought about a rapid expansion of Operation Vanguard. In 1964, there were ten agricultural demonstration teams in Africa.[275] Between 1961 and 1974, ROC agricultural missions were reported to have worked in twenty-three countries, with over nine hundred technicians winning friendship and admiration from their hosts.[276] There were also seminars held in Taiwan to train Africans.[277] While the effectiveness of the ROC assistance in reducing poverty and hunger in Africa

---

270 Shinn and Eisenman, 2012: 27–29.
271 Jiang, 2016: 90.
272 Gao, 1993: 78.
273 Wei, 1978: 326–328.
274 Liu, 2007: 161–181.
275 Wei, 1978: 334.
276 Wei, 1978: 338–341.
277 Wei, 1978: 343–351.

remained questionable, the ROC evidently received from Africa political support in the United Nations during the 1960s. What is more, in aiding the underdeveloped black Africans, the Chinese in Taiwan regained the feeling of superiority, thus strengthening Taipei's claim to be the legitimate China.[278]

To be sure, the ROC has been eager to garner support from the African countries. Taipei was willing to compromise, as the case of Mongolia's admission to the United Nations shows. In 1961, the Soviet Union threatened to block the admission of Mauritania if that of Mongolia was failed again. Representatives from several African states informed the ROC ambassador to the United Nations Jiang Tingfu that if he vetoed the application of Mongolia this time again, they would seek to replace Taipei with Beijing.[279] Such a development caused concerns in both Taipei and Washington. In behind-the-scenes communication, Jiang Jieshi promised not to veto the admission of Mongolia. In return, Kennedy made an assurance that the United States would use its veto, if needed at any time, to prevent Chinese Communist entry into the United Nations.[280] Though compromised on this issue, Jiang never meant to grant recognition to Mongolia, for he could not afford to lose the territory while claiming to be the legitimate ruler of China. In the end, Jiang did not participate in the vote on Mongolia's membership. As a result, the General Assembly adopted the resolution on October 27, 1961, admitting Mongolia into the United Nations.[281] Ironically, holding the China's seat in the United Nations does not necessarily strengthen Taipei's position.

Overall, Taipei's status in the international arena declined as more and more states recognized Beijing. The establishment of diplomatic relations between France and the PRC on January 27, 1964 was known as the diplomatic nuclear bomb that shocked the Chinese on the island.[282] Taipei was notified in advance, but it protested in vain. Understanding Charles de Gaulle as someone "almost impossible to persuade," Taipei's personnel eventually left Paris in February and made way for Beijing.[283] From time to time, there were voices calling for the

278 Liu, 2012: 141–171.
279 Jiang Tingfu voted against the admission of Mongolia in 1955, arguing that Mongolia was not an independent sovereign state, but a part of China stolen by the Soviet Union. This was the only veto casted by the ROC during its possession of China's seat in the Security Council. Clark II, 2018: 263–295.
280 Keefer, et al., 1996: 156.
281 United Nations General Assembly, 1961a.
282 Zhai, 2012: 14–27.
283 Schwar, 1998: 11.

recognition of both the PRC and the ROC, which were ardently opposed from both sides of the Taiwan Strait. In an extreme case, in Dahomey, where diplomatic relations were complicated by internal turmoil during 1964–1966, two Chinese embassies existed at the same time for nearly half a year. Some observers took it as the precedence for dual recognition, while the ROC officials resisted such an idea.[284]

During the 1960s, there were also several "two Chinas" proposals made in the United Nations, but any draft resolution containing such an idea could mobilize enough votes due to the shared rejection from Taipei and Beijing.[285] In 1970, it has been made clear that the present of the PRC was inevitable, and it was impossible to keep a seat for Taipei's representative either as China or as Taiwan.[286] On October 25, 1971, by an overwhelming majority of 76–35 with seventeen abstentions, the General Assembly adopted the Albanian sponsored resolution to "restore all its rights to the People's Republic of China and to recognize the representatives of its Government as the only legitimate representative of China to the United Nations, and to expel forthwith the representatives of Chiang Kai-shek [Jiang Jieshi] from the place which they unlawfully occupy at the United Nations and in all the organizations related to it."[287] Anticipating that, the ROC delegation walked out before the vote was taken. Be it withdrawal or expulsion from the world organization, it unveiled Taipei's fall into international limbo.

Many people criticized Jiang Jieshi's foreign policy as inflexible and questioned the position of "both cannot coexist in the same place."[288] Gao Lang argues that "both cannot coexist in the same place" was not the cause for the diplomatic failure but rather an excuse.[289] Indeed, in such a competition, it would prove to be in vain even Taipei accepted dual recognition as long as Beijing's stance remained the same. Jiang Jieshi could be confident that Mao Zedong would not accept a two-China arrangement, and however different these two

---

284 Wang, 2009: 151–190.
285 Gao, 1993: 216–217.
286 Luard, 1971: 729–744.
287 United Nations General Assembly, 1971.
288 In Chinese: Han zei bu liang li. Quoted from Zhuge Liang's famous work *Later Chu Shi Biao*. In this article, Zhuge, Shu Han chancellor, made it clear he would devote all his life to recover the rightful territory of Han dynasty stolen by Cao Wei. Zhuge eventually died during his expedition against Wei. In contrast, Jiang Jieshi never got such a chance.
289 Gao, 1993: 40.

longtime life-and-death enemies were, they shared the commitment to the territorial integrity of China.[290]

Undoubtedly, the exclusion from the United Nations and other international organizations, and the termination of diplomatic ties with dozens of countries during the 1970s forced Taipei into international isolation. Taipei's self-identification as the sole legitimate government of China was shattered. Jiang Jingguo[291] tried to bring Taipei back onto the international stage with pragmatic diplomacy, to expand commercial, cultural, technological and sports relationships without re-identifying the ROC. As a result, Taipei could participate in various international organizations such as the World Trade Organization, the Asia-Pacific Economic Cooperation, and also Olympic Games with the name "Chinese Taipei."

Unlike his father's preparation to retake the mainland, Jiang Jingguo focused on the economic construction on the island, and the localization of the KMT and the government. The tension across the Taiwan Strait was lessened, and family visits to the mainland were firstly allowed in 1987.

After Jiang Jingguo's sudden death in 1988, Li Denghui became the first Taiwan-born president. He proposed to negotiate cross-strait issues on a special state-to-state relationship, which was furiously denounced by Beijing. In the meanwhile, he attempted to break Taipei out of the diplomatic limbo by frequent foreign visits. This effort, however, has yielded no real diplomatic gains and has only provoked a violent reaction from the mainland.

After the end of martial law, Taipei gradually re-identified itself on democratic values. However, it is argued that those who (re-)recognized Taipei after 1988 had little to do with regime types.[292]

Summary

As bluntly pointed out by Ralph Clough, the competition for international recognition between Beijing and Taipei was unequal, for the PRC clearly qualified as the government of China by most customary tests.[293] During the 1950s and 1960s, Taipei was able to buttress its position mainly because of its alliance with the United States and its occupation of China's seat in the United Nations. As an

---

290 Mao, 1998: 297; Taylor, 2009: 501.
291 Jiang Jieshi's son, who served as the head of the Executive Yuan since 1972, and became the President in 1978.
292 Hu, 2015: 22–23.
293 Clough, 1978: 154.

important episode of the Détente, the United States raised no more hurdles to prevent the People's Republic from the international community, and granted the long-postponed recognition to Beijing. In the 1970s, most countries switched their allegiance to Beijing (see Figure 5-3).

Throughout this diplomatic warfare between Beijing and Taipei, their shared commitment to One-China principle has been the most striking feature, which makes any form of dual-recognition impossible. No matter how ideologically different apart, the CCP and the KMT are committed to getting rid of the humiliation suffered under the great powers, and achieving the prosperity of the Chinese nation. The Civil War between them has never been officially finished, but only frozen by the United States; therefore, the diplomatic competition between the PRC and the ROC is a logical continuation. Both the PRC and the ROC claim to be the only lawful representative of Chinese people, and desire to be recognized accordingly.

As it turned out, the Cold War logic dominated in the starting period, while in the long run, the principle of effectiveness prevailed.

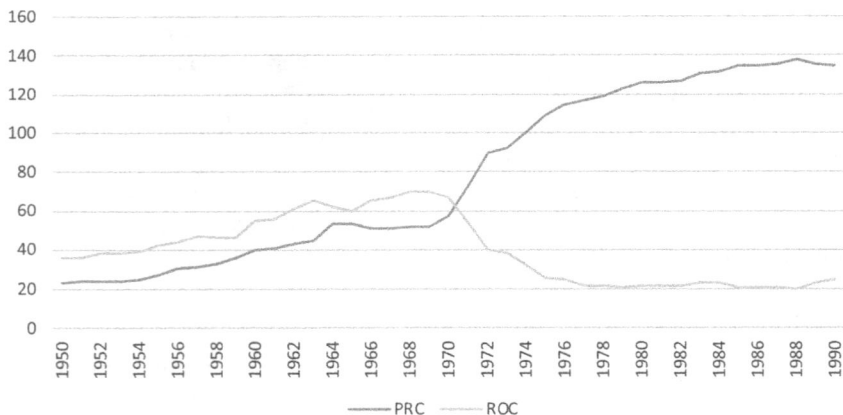

Figure 5-3. China: Diplomatic Recognition, 1950–1990

Meanwhile, Newnham argues that after being deserted by the West, the ROC was relatively successful in purchasing recognition under extremely unfavorable conditions.[294] Indeed, ever since the launch of the Operation Vanguard, Taipei

294 Newnham, 2000: 273.

has implicitly or explicitly connected aid to recognition. After its economic takeoff – as one of the Four Little Dragons – Taipei has gained a strong base for economic diplomacy, and its struggle to buy diplomatic recognition continues actively to this day. In all, Taipei's dollar diplomacy turns to be more attractive to these small states with weak economy lying hundreds of miles away.[295] However, with the rise of China, the island's economic success is overshadowed. Once again, time is not on Taipei's side.[296] Understanding the importance of economic factors – and foreign aid in particular – I refrain from including them in this research for two main reasons: first, the statistics are considered to be state secrets, therefore hardly accessible;[297] second, some data are incomparable.

In short, the island is dwarfed by the mainland. Taipei remains internationally marginalized. Would it be better to sentence the death of the ROC and declare an independent Taiwan? The answer seems to be a clear no. As long as Beijing adheres to the One-China principle, there is no way for Taipei's re-identification to be recognized.

5.2. Germany

From Occupation to Partition

The division of Germany is both a reason for and a result of the Cold War. Germany's future was determined by the Allies before its unconditional surrender in May 1945. Germany was split into four military occupation zones, administered by the Soviet Union, the United States, the United Kingdom, and France, respectively. Berlin would be a special area under joint occupation of the four powers. The Allied Control Council, consisting of the commanders-in-chief of the four zones, was the supreme authority, in charge of matters affecting Germany as a whole. The Allies had determined their general lines toward Germany as denazification, demilitarization, democratization, and decentralization.

Starting from 1946, a series of agreements between the Americans and British launched the economic fusion of their zones, which merged into the Bizonia on January 1, 1947. Their military governors worked cautiously to make sure this was only an economic union, not a political one, as the latter was thought to hurt

---

295 Rich, 2009: 177–178; Hu, 2015: 2–3.
296 Payne and Veney, 2001: 448; Rich and Banerjee, 2015: 157.
297 Brautigam, 2009: 12.

the chances for reunification.[298] On June 5, 1947, the United States announced a European Recovery Program, also known as Marshall Plan, which marked a fundamental shift in American policy toward Europe and signaled the full-fledged onset of the Cold War. The Bizonia and then the French zone were included in the Marshall Plan. The economic potential of Germany was essential for the European economic reconstruction. As George Kennan put it clearly, "To talk about the recovery of Europe and to oppose the recovery of Germany is nonsense. People can have both or they can have neither."[299] However, a new German economy could not be effectively integrated into the European economy without a proper German government, as the Americans realized that the Marshall Plan "would remain incomplete as long as Germany was unable to speak for itself to other nations and in this respect remained dependent on the military governments."[300] Some form of a German government had to be created. In March 1948, the United States, the United Kingdom, France, and the Benelux countries agreed upon the establishment of a federal democratic government in the Bizonia and the French zone. Therefore, the Marshall Plan became the turning point of the post-war Germany, leading Western Germany from an occupied territory to a sovereign state.[301]

As the Soviet representative withdrew from the ACC in March 1948, the quadripartite apparatus was never able to be revived. The cooperation between the war-time Allies broke down completely. There would be more than one Germany. The process to create a separate German state accelerated. To create an economically stable Western Germany, a currency reform was required. On June 21, 1948, the military authorities of the three Western zones introduced a new currency, the deutsche mark, to replace the terribly inflated Reichsmark. The introduction of the deutsche mark in the Western zones in itself was an apparent violation of the Potsdam Accord, according to which Germany would be treated as a single economic unit.[302] What is more, the new currency was considered to be a concrete measure of separation of Western Germany. Stalin counteracted by stopping the exchange of goods and blockading all access to Western Berlin. The West responded with a remarkable airlift, and counter-blockaded the essential industrial materials to the Soviet occupation zone. As a result, the Berlin

---

298 Maulucci, 2012: 49.
299 Cited in Miller, 2000: 16.
300 Schwabe, 1991: 250.
301 Thomaneck and Niven, 2001: 16.
302 Thomaneck and Niven, 2001: 34.

Blockade became a symbol of Soviet repression and inhumanity, coupled with the Berlin Airlift as an icon of Western commitment to freedom. Pro-Western feelings prevailed among the Germans, especially the Berliners.

Meanwhile, the German Minister-Presidents were asked by the Western Allies to comply with the plan to merge the three Western zones into one political, economic, and constitutional unit. The Parliamentary Council chaired by Konrad Adenauer was set up in Bonn in September 1948, to draft a new constitution for a new German government. *The Basic Law of the Federal Republic of Germany* was worked out on May 8, 1949, and the term "constitution" was carefully avoided by the Germans for a permanent constitution should wait until sovereignty and unification came.[303] On May 12, the day the Berlin Blockade lifted, three military governors approved this constitution. On May 23, 1949, the Basic Law entered into force, which marked the establishment of the Federal Republic of Germany.

In the meanwhile, the communists were consolidating their control in East Germany. The Socialist Unity Party of Germany was established in Berlin in April 1946, by the merging of the Communist Party and the Social Democratic Party. The SED gradually took control of the civilian administration in the zone. Moreover, in 1948, they began to build a new police force, the People's Police, which was interpreted by the West as the foundation for a new German army. As the establishment of the Federal Republic in the Western zones, Stalin had no other choice but to approve to build a government in the Soviet zone. On October 7, 1949, the German Democratic Republic came into being. In his first government statement on October 12, Otto Grotewohl, the Prime Minister, pronounced that the GDR was willing "to establish peaceful and friendly relations with all states, that were prepared to live in peace and friendship with Germany and recognized our national interests."[304] The Soviets and their allies quickly commenced formal diplomatic relations with the GDR, as listed in Table 5-3.

---

303 Feldkamp, 2008.
304 Küsters, 1996: 190–198.

Table 5-3. Communist Bloc's Recognition of the GDR

Country	Date
Soviet Union	1949.10.15
Bulgaria	1949.10.17
Poland	1949.10.18
Czechoslovakia	1949.10.18
Hungary	1949.10.19
Romania	1949.10.22
China, PR	1949.10.25
Korea, DPR	1949.11.07
Albania	1949.12.02
Vietnam, DR	1950.02.03
Mongolia	1950.04.13

Nonetheless, as insisted by Stalin, the new government was labeled as "provisional," and its geographic area was not specified in its constitution. While the GDR leaders were devoted to building a separate communist German state, their boss in Moscow preferred to keeping the question open.

Who should be responsible for this division? The attitudes of the four powers towards Germany varied from each other. To draw a spectrum from division to unification, the French would no doubt stand at the end of division. Traumatized by the war, the French saw a resurgent Germany as the prominent threat to Europe. With its economic and military potential, a united Germany would be unstoppable. Dominated by the Germanophobia, there was a wide-spread agreement in France that the more fragmented Germany is, the safer France will be. Nonetheless, the French were too weak to make this happen. As the tension between the two superpowers intensified, "French policy towards Germany was gradually reduced to nothing in the face of Anglo-Saxon objectives."[305]

The British view was more complicated. Like the French, they did not trust the Germans, but judged the Soviets to be more dangerous. By early 1946, there had emerged a cold-war mentality in London. Encountering the Soviet expansionism, a Germany – if not united, then at least the western part – was needed to redress the balance of power.[306] However, the British could not act alone this time.

---

305 Girault, 1986: 51.
306 Deighton, 1990: 224.

Carolyn W. Eisenberg argues that "the division of Germany was fundamentally an American decision."[307] The Americans were committed to create a political and economic system, which was in contrast to the Soviet world view, and the German productive capacity was the keystone of the European political economy.[308] The American policy makers opted for division so that they could more effectively deal with matters in the West. The course was set with the Marshall Plan. Since then, the Americans cooperated with the British and French toward a separate West Germany integrated into the economic recovery of Europe, and later also defense.

The Soviet Union was not interested in the division of Germany at all. Stalin was of the conviction that national unity was far more important to the Germans than their political system.[309] Stalin wanted no GDR, as Wilfried Loth argues, it is Walter Ulbricht who should take the main responsibility for the real existence of a socialist GDR.[310] In a purely power-politic sense, the Soviets had firm control over their zone anyway. Therefore, if Germany remained united, the Soviets could only gain more influence over the rest.[311] Even after 1949, Stalin still saw the German question as unfixed. Regardless of his motivations, Stalin pushed for the reunification of Germany harder than other leaders.[312]

Germany was of great geostrategic importance. It was only too important that neither the East nor the West could accept the possibility of a united Germany aligned with the other bloc. As noticed by Hermann-Josef Rupieper, the West needed West Germany and would not leave it to the Germans, let alone the East. Therefore, the German question was never put to the Germans.[313] In the meantime, a united and independent Germany would threaten everyone. A divided Germany was the second-best choice tolerable for all interested powers.

---

307 Eisenberg, 1996: 9.
308 Kuklick, 1972.
309 Orlow, 2006: 538.
310 Loth, 1994: 226–228.
311 Thomaneck and Niven, 2001: 23.
312 There have been heated discussions on the intentions and goals among historians, but no consensus on the Stalin Note has been reached. See Ruggenthaler, 2015: 197–199.
313 Rupieper, 1986: 427–428.

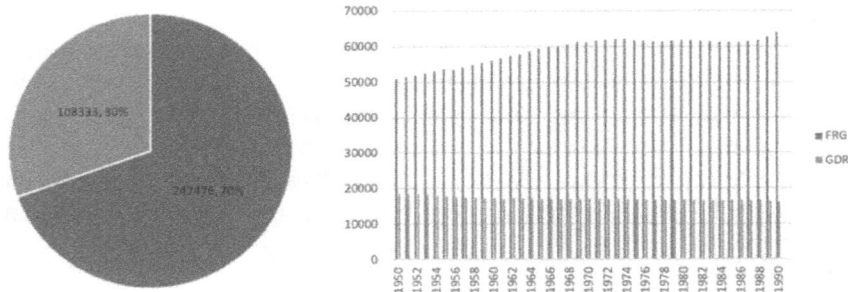

Figure 5-4. Germany: Area and Population

For sure, the division is uneven. The GDR's area was less than half that of the FRG. Together, they made up of three quarters of the pre-war German territory – those territories east of the Oder-Neisse line were acquired by Poland and the Soviet Union. And the German population in these areas were expelled, which was justified under the desire of ethnically homogeneous nation-states. Because of the performance of Nazi, a German minority was viewed as troublesome in Central and Eastern Europe. It was estimated that some eight million expellees fled to the FRG by 1950, while approximately four million settled in the GDR – the expellees constituted over 20 % of the total population at that time.[314] The massive movement of the German population continued until the construction of the Berlin Wall in 1961, and more than three million East Germans fled to the West. After that, the East German population gradually stabilized, which was roughly a quarter of that of the Federal Republic, as shown in Figure 5-4.

In addition, the FRG was founded in the most developed part of Germany. After analyzing electoral results during the Weimar Republic, Michael Bernhard argues that the western part had a greater democratic potential than that in the east, which is a significant factor in the democratization of the FRG.[315]

Indeed, the Federal Republic has been built into a viable democracy, which gets full marks in Polity IV, as shown in Figure 5-5. In contrast, the GDR was an autocracy that scored even lower than other socialist countries. During the 1950s and 1960s, the Western refused to recognize the GDR on the ground that it was created without free elections, therefore not in accordance with democratic standards.[316]

---

314 Ahonen, 2003: 1–2.
315 Bernhard, 2001: 381–383.
316 Crawford, 2006: 456.

Nevertheless, they were not consistent in practice – all of them recognized the GDR in the 1970s, when East Berlin made no attempt to democratize according to their standards.

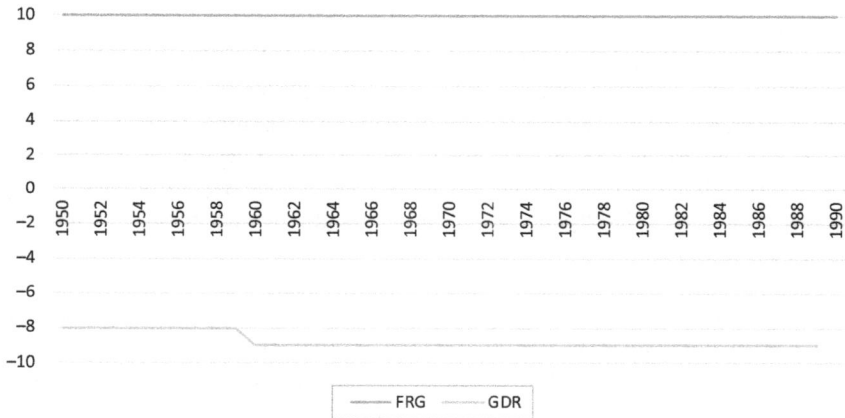

Figure 5-5. Germany: Polity Scores

The FRG

Emerging from occupation in 1949, the FRG was by no means a sovereign state. According to the Occupation Statute, certain crucial fields were reserved under the control of the Allied High Commission, including matters related to the Basic Law, foreign trade, and foreign affairs.[317]

On September 15, 1949, Konrad Adenauer was elected Chancellor. His foreign policy was focused on incorporation of the FRG into the West, attainment of sovereignty, maintenance of a pro-American political orientation, and European unity with the Franco-German reconciliation as the core.[318]

The proclamation of the GDR raised concerns in the West. On October 21, Adenauer claimed in front of the Bundestag that the establishment of the GDR was imposed by the Soviet Union instead of the free will of the German people. He further announced that the FRG was the only legitimate government authorized to speak for the German people, which also included the Germans

---

317 United States Department of States, 1985: 213.
318 Maulucci, 2012: 101.

in the SBZ, until the accomplishment of German unity.[319] The FRG's claim to be the sole representative of the entire German people, known in German as *Alleinvertretungsanspruch*, was the principle guiding its foreign policy in the next two decades.

It has been agreed that the German unification was never Adenauer's priority. To some extent, he was of the conviction that the Eastern part was gone for good.[320] But he would not openly air his lack of interest in reunification, for there was a strong calling for a united Germany both within and outside his party.[321] Adenauer's tactic was to propose unacceptable preconditions and let the East Germans and their Soviet patron to bear the burden. By doing so, he successfully won the support of the expellee groups and strengthened his position in the bargain with the Allies.[322]

The process to normalcy accelerated with the escalation of the East-West conflict, and the first breakthrough came in November, when Adenauer signed agreements with the AHC on the Petersberg. They agreed that their primary object was the integration of the FRG as a peaceful member of the European community. To this end, the FRG was permitted to re-establish consular and commercial relations with other countries.[323] As a result, the Occupation Statute was revised, and the Federal Foreign Office was re-established later on March 15, 1951, with Chancellor Adenauer as the first Foreign Minister. Those representatives accredited to the AHC immediately transformed into diplomatic missions to the FRG. Thereafter, the FRG began to play an active role in the international community.

The process to gain sovereignty was further sped up as the war broke out in Korea. According to the Western perception of a communist monolithium, the North Korean leaders seemed to act as Kremlin's puppets. Americans and Europeans noticed parallels between divided Germany and divided Korea. Fears grew, for the possibility that the Soviets might build up the East Germans and invade westward. Adenauer was convinced that "Stalin had planned the same tactic he had applied in Korea in the case of West Germany."[324] At that time, West Germany was defenseless, as a consequence of the disarmament and demilitarization process after 1945. In addition, it was neither a member of, nor under

---

319 Küsters, 1996: 212–216.
320 Ahonen, 2003: 86–87.
321 Marcussen, et al., 1999: 623–624; Kleuters, 2012: 26–34.
322 Ahonen, 2003: 91–93.
323 United States Department of States, 1985: 310–313.
324 Adenauer, 1965: 349.

the protection of the North Atlantic Treaty Organization, which was originally planned to provide defense along the Rhine. An expansionist Soviet Union at this juncture overtook a resurgent Germany as the most dangerous threat to peace. Consequently, West Germany became a potential partner instead of a menace. Just as the German economic potential was critical to the reconstruction of European economy, the German manpower was indispensable to the defense of Europe. Shocked by events in Korea, the rearmament of Germany suddenly became acceptable and inevitable. The Korean War paved the way for the FRG to become a NATO member.[325]

In order for the FRG to join the NATO, the occupation status had to be completely altered. Three Western Foreign Ministers formally endorsed the FRG's sole representative claim in September 1950.[326] In the *Communiqué on Germany*, they declared that "the three Governments consider the Government of the Federal Republic as the only German Government freely and legitimately constituted and therefore entitled to speak for Germany as the representative of the German people in international affairs."[327] This position was further included in the Paris Agreements, and was therefore accepted by all the NATO members. The Paris Agreements, eventually signed in October 1954, announced the termination of the three Western powers' occupation of Germany, the abolition of the AHC, and the restoration of sovereignty to the FRG.[328] After the agreements had been ratified by all involved parties, the FRG became a sovereign state, and a member of NATO on May 5, 1955. Thus, the rearmament issue "resulted in sovereignty, international recognition, and the preservation of freedom for West Germany."[329]

The year 1955 marked a watershed in the post-war Germany. The four-power occupation ended; sovereignty restored, but not to one Germany. As two German

---

325 The issue of German rearmament had already discussed and approved by the Americans and the British. However, the French opposition was only overcome by an imminent Soviet threat after the breakout of Korean War. For a detailed discussion, see Hrdlicka, 1990: 276–301.

326 Adenauer wrote to the AHC asking for their support of the claim but was ignored. In diplomatic practice, the Western Allies were in line with the non-recognition of the GDR, and persuaded others in their sphere of influence to do so. See Küsters, 1996: 233; Scholz, 2006: 558.

327 Stauffer, et al., 1977: 1297.

328 The Allies reserved their rights and responsibilities concerning Berlin and Germany as a whole until 1990.

329 Hrdlicka, 1990: 295.

states integrated tightly into two opposing blocs respectively, the unification of Germany was postponed indefinitely.

The Soviets were among the very first to accept the de facto co-existence of two German states. Unlike Stalin's insistence on the pursuit of German unity, Nikita Khrushchev proposed the two-state theory. The Soviet Union was ready to open diplomatic relations with the FRG, and to push for the recognition of the GDR. Subsequently, as invited by the Soviets, Adenauer paid a state visit to Moscow in September 1955. The negotiation turned out to be difficult. Nevertheless, Adenauer and Khrushchev agreed upon the establishment of diplomatic relations and exchange ambassadors between Bonn and Moscow. Hence, the Soviet Union became the very first country to have diplomatic relations with both German states, and it remained to be the only one for a rather long period.

As a result of Adenauer's visit, there would be two German ambassadors in Moscow representing two separate German governments, one from Bonn, and the other from East Berlin. Would this situation be interpreted as the FRG no longer insisting on its exclusive mandate? What if others follow the example set by the Soviet Union to build diplomatic relations with both the FRG and the GDR?[330] This would no doubt undermine the credibility of Bonn's policy on reunification. On the flight back to Bonn, Wilhelm Grewe proposed that a third country's recognition of the GDR as a sovereign state would be an unfriendly act against the FRG, for it would lead to further division of Germany and hinder the FRGs' pursuit of reunification. Such a thought was expanded further, known as Hallstein Doctrine.[331] Addressing the Bundestag on September 22, Adenauer stated that "in relation to third states, we will continue to maintain our existing standpoint concerning the so-called German Democratic Republic. I must unambiguously emphasize that the Federal Government will continue to consider the opening of diplomatic relations with the GDR by third states with whom she maintains official relations as an unfriendly act, as this would deepen the division of Germany."[332]

In Adenauer's justification, the Soviet Union was an exception on account of its status as a signature to the Potsdam Agreements, who had rights and responsibilities for Berlin and for Germany as a whole. Nevertheless, such an argument

---

330 It was mainly targeted on the East Europeans and the neutralists. See Grewe, 1979: 251.
331 Named after Walter Hallstien, the State Secretary at the Foreign Office. It was first used as "Hallstein-Grewe Doctrine" by Joachim Schwelien in his article published in the *Frankfurter Allgemeine Zeitung*, July 5, 1958. See Gray, 2003: 84–85.
332 Deuerlein, 1961: 401–402.

of exceptionalism was not well heard abroad. As already shown in Bandung, the majority of Asian and African countries had no specific position towards the German problem. Instead of choosing sides, they preferred to recognize both Bonn and East Berlin.[333] Even inside the Western bloc, there were different voices. Denmark, for instance, a NATO state, considered itself to be a special case for it was the only one neighboring to both the FRG and the GDR.[334]

To prevent international recognition of the GDR, more concrete measures were required. In an FRG ambassadors' conference in December 1955, Foreign Minister Heinrich von Brentano took a tough line, instructing that the FRG would not open diplomatic relations with East European satellite states, and the FRG would terminate its relations with any third state that recognized the GDR as a sovereign state.[335] Brentano further reiterated his view when he declared his foreign policy in front of the Bundestag in June 1956. Thus, the Hallstein Doctrine eventually transformed into a proactive policy.[336]

When it cut off its diplomatic relations with Belgrade in 1957, Bonn showed that it was unquestionably serious about this policy. It was made public on October 15, 1957 that Yugoslavia would commence diplomatic relations with the GDR. From the Yugoslavs point of view, the recognition of the GDR was a logical continuation of their non-aligned policy. It simply acknowledged the fact that there were two German states existing on German soil, which should not be interpreted as an act against the FRG, but "Yugoslavia's contribution to a peaceful settlement of the German problem."[337] In contrast, the West Germans and their allies understood the recognition of the GDR as a challenge to Bonn's position, a concession to the Soviets pressure, and even more, a symbol of Yugoslavia's alignment with the Soviet bloc. And according to Brentano's estimation, if Bonn took no retaliation, it would lead to 25–35 countries following the Yugoslavia's example.[338] Thus, on October 18, the FRG terminated its diplomatic relations with Yugoslavia – "a real slap in the face to Tito."[339] The Yugoslavs were caught by surprise. They did expect some sort of sanctions but did not expected a complete break in diplomatic relations. If the Yugoslavs misjudged because the West

333 Kilian, 2001: 368; Das Gupta, 2019: 115.
334 Lammers, 2006: 453–472.
335 Booz, 1995: 28.
336 Kleuters, 2012: 60; Gray, 2003: 44–49; Kilian, 2001: 24–25.
337 DiGangi, et al., 1992: 786.
338 Kilian, 2001: 57.
339 To quote the phrase of the British Foreign Secretary Selwyn Lloyd, DiGangi, et al., 1992: 788.

Germans never explicitly warned them about it, then after the breakoff of Yugo-West German relations, no one would question the seriousness of the Hallstein Doctrine.[340] In hindsight, the implementation of the Hallstein Doctrine on Yugoslavia successfully prevented several countries from recognizing the GDR as a sovereign state for more than a decade.

By the mid of 1950s, the FRG had regained its economic strength, therefore capable of making a major contribution to the development of the Third World. Although the West Germans were reluctant in the beginning, they were "pushed to the front" by their Western allies.[341] Without colonial ties, the FRG could direct its resources to where they were most needed, which no doubt added the credibility of its economic assistance. As it turned out, African and Asian countries learned that it would be more profitable to choose the FRG.[342] Through providing bilateral aid to the geo-strategically significant countries – mainly India, Pakistan, Turkey, Chile, and Iran – the FRG strengthened its political status in the international community.[343]

In the meanwhile, the Federal Republic adopted the Wilsonian catchword self-determination to the German question, likening the GDR as a colony under the oppression of the Soviet Union. Emphasizing this universal principle would no doubt generate more sympathies in the Third World than a specific German demand on reunification.[344] The Western allies, as the former colonial masters, facilitated Bonn's non-recognition policy and prevented any East German presence in their spheres of influence. At the same time, once a colony gained independence, Bonn would immediately announce its recognition of the new state and establish a diplomatic mission in the capital.[345]

Some politicians in Bonn equated the East-West rivalry to the Arab-Israeli conflict. At that time, there were no official relations between the FRG and Israel. On the one hand, Bonn was unenthusiastic, fearing of irritating the Arab countries and pushing them to the GDR side. On the other hand, the Israelis had no trust in the Germans. As the Soviets supported Nasser's Egypt, the FRG – sometimes under the US pressure for burden-sharing – increased its financial and military assistance to Israel in the early 1960s.[346]

---

340 Maricic, 2019: 65.
341 Schmidt, 2003: 473.
342 Winrow, 1990: 42–46.
343 von Bressensdorf and Seefried, 2017: 12.
344 Gray, 2003: 103.
345 Gray, 2003: 104.
346 Trentin, 2009: 499.

In 1965, Nasser invited Ulbricht to Egypt, and threatened the West Germans that Egypt would recognize the GDR if the FRG continued transferring arms and providing aids to Israel. Although short of diplomatic recognition, Ulbricht was received in Egypt with full state honors throughout the visit from February 24 to March 1, 1965. Ulbricht's visit was read as a major psychological victory over the FRG, and *Neues Deutschland* boldly announced that the Hallstein Doctrine was bankrupt.[347]

Bonn retaliated. Hardliners, such as the former Chancellor Adenauer, called for invoking the Hallstein Doctrine and breaking off diplomatic relations with Egypt. Erhard chose to cancel the impeding aid programs in Egypt and open diplomatic relations with Israel. After two-month-long negotiations, Bonn and Tel Aviv formally established diplomatic relations on May 13, 1965.[348] The Arab League members, with the exception of Morocco, Tunisia and Libya, severed diplomatic relations with the FRG at once. However, none of them recognized the GDR. The Arab states were reluctant to commit themselves to the Soviet bloc by granting diplomatic recognition to the GDR. Even the progressive Arab states would make use of the recognition of the GDR "as a ransom in order to obtain a maximum of military aid and political and economic support."[349] In the meanwhile, the West German development aids to the Arab world continued, which ensured Bonn's leverage.[350]

Generally speaking, the Hallstein Doctrine functioned well during Adenauer's period, even though more and more voices questioned its stubbornness and worried about being blackmailed. This policy would face a great challenge from inside as the West German Social Democrats entered the government in 1966. The Social Democrats developed the concept of "Change through Rapprochement" (*Wandel durch Annäherung*) since the beginning of the 1960s.[351] Serving as the mayor of West Berlin from 1957 to 1966, Willy Brandt had to deal with the East in a more pragmatic manner. In December 1966, the popular mayor of West Berlin took office as Vice Chancellor and Foreign Minister of the Grand Coalition, and his idea of rapprochement found its way to the federal level. In Chancellor Kiesinger's first declaration of policy before the Bundestag on December 13, the new government stated that it would improve human, economic and cultural relations with the other side,

347 *Neues Deutschland*, March 9, 1965, 1.
348 Fink, 2019: 19–22.
349 Gray, 2003: 202.
350 Winrow, 1990: 70.
351 Kleuters, 2012: 20.

to relax tensions instead of hardening them, overcome trenches instead of deepening them.[352] Furthermore, during another parliament session, Kiesinger made it clear that his government would tackle practical matters and make the division of Germany as painless as possible since the solution of German question remained impossible for the time being.[353] However, relations with the East Germans were refrained to a technical level, which means that, by and large, the Grand Coalition's policy did not deviate from the principle of sole representation and non-recognition of the GDR.[354]

On January 31, 1967, Romania established diplomatic relations with the FRG, and the common communique was silent on the recognition of a second German state, simply ignoring the problem of the Hallstein Doctrine.[355] Romania was an easy task, although a Warsaw Pact member state, it had already demonstrated a certain degree of autonomy under Nicolae Ceausescu's leadership.[356] The FRG justified its move in accordance with the birth defect theory, which argued that the Soviets forced the Eastern European socialist countries to cement diplomatic relations with the GDR, and thus they could not be blamed for these actions.[357] On the other side, *Neues Deutschland* commented that the establishment of West German-Romanian relations did not mean the end of the Hallstein Doctrine, for the core of this doctrine was the sole representativeness. Moreover, the Romanians were accused of violating the Warsaw Pact's declaration made in Bucharest on July 12, 1966.[358] In response, the Romanians accused the East Germans of intervening in their internal affairs.[359] Ostensibly, Bonn's Ostpolitik drove a wedge between the East Germans and their socialist brothers.

Bonn and Belgrade re-established diplomatic relations on January 31, 1968. The rapprochement did not encounter any serious interruption from East Berlin. On the contrary, the GDR welcomed this development, which was interpreted as a piece of definite evidence that the Hallstein Doctrine was bankrupt.[360] Now what remained of the Hallstein Doctrine after the reconciliation between the FRG and Yugoslavia? "Although Bonn still claimed the validity of the Hallstein

---

352 Oberländer, 1984: 60.
353 Oberländer, 1984: 1281.
354 Oberländer, 1984: 60.
355 Oberländer, 1984: 430–431.
356 Stanciu, 2014: 117.
357 Kilian, 2001: 337.
358 *Neues Deutschland*, February 3, 1967, 1.
359 Oberländer, 1984: 479.
360 Maricic, 2019: 260.

Doctrine," as pointed out by Alan Maricic, "the reestablishment of relations with Yugoslavia showed that it had run its course."[361] Observers predicted a wave of recognition of the GDR, which is surely what the East Germans had been hoping for. Bonn launched a worldwide covering operation, explaining the Grand Coalition's foreign policy, and pleading other countries not to take advantage of this situation by recognizing the GDR. The operation worked smoothly among leading non-aligned countries. As asserted by Gray, "by 1968 it seemed unlikely that the GDR would ever win substantial international recognition on its own strength."[362]

At the same time, Bonn by no means stopped expanding and deepening economic ties with the socialist states, hoping for peaceful change. The Soviets invasion in Czechoslovakia and suppression of the Prague Spring in August 1968 came as a shock to those in Bonn. It had been made clear that the discipline of the socialist camp must be maintained, and the improvement of East-West relations had to be centered in Moscow.[363] Bonn had to focus on direct negotiation with Moscow and prepare to make more concessions to ease the Soviets feeling of uncertainty. To this end, the recognition of the status quo in Europe was the very first step. The Social Democrats came to the conclusion that the existence of the GDR had to be recognized in a certain form; however, the time was not yet ripe since there were still strong opposition from their coalition partner – the conservative Christian Democrats.

A further blow came from the Third World. On April 30, 1969, Iraq announced that it would establish diplomatic relations with the GDR. On May 8, Cambodia made a similar announcement. Shortly after, Sudan, Syria, South Yemen, and Egypt respectively recognized the GDR. Since the Arab states already broke off their relations with the FRG in 1965, Bonn could not invoke the Hallstein Doctrine to punish these unfriendly acts. Yet, the Grand Coalition disputed over whether to terminate the Cambodian-West German relations, established only in November 1967, or not. How to handle the Cambodia's case reflected disagreements over the German question, which was intensified as the election was coming. Chancellor Kiesinger and his fellow Christian Democrats preferred strong action, which met resistance from Brandt's Foreign Office. The coalition split, and no decisions were made, except of canceling all projected aids to Cambodia. From the Cambodian perspective, entertaining diplomatic relations

361 Maricic, 2019: 263.
362 Gray, 2003: 204.
363 Niedhart, 2016: 29.

with the GDR was merely a restoration of its balance on the German question, as demanded by the principle of neutrality.[364] However, the Cambodian felt offended by the West German "great power chauvinism," and turned to the Soviets for compensation.[365] In the end, Prince Sihanouk announced to break diplomatic relations with the FRG on June 11. The wave of recognizing the GDR halted in July. To a certain extent, this was a relief to both Bonn and East Berlin – while the West Germans feared a foreign policy's catastrophe, the East Germans simply could not afford to buy more foreign friends.[366] The East-West German diplomatic warfare was approaching an end.

In October 1969, the social-liberal coalition replaced the Grand Coalition, with Willy Brandt took office as the Chancellor and Walter Scheel as the Foreign Minister. In dealing with the GDR, Brandt's approach was to recognize the GDR as a state, but not a foreign country. However, the new government, instead of giving up the old doctrine right away, continued to discourage third states from dealing with the GDR as a normal state. Without doubt, Brandt would benefit from (renouncing) the Hallstein Doctrine. During the German-German negotiations, Brandt tactically used it as a means of keeping up the pressure on Ulbricht, and later Honecker, which turned out to be "simply too useful as a source of leverage over the SED regime."[367]

Eventually, on December 17, 1972, the FRG and the GDR signed the Basic Treaty, recognized each other as sovereign states, and agreed to establish permanent missions. Bonn sent its first permanent representative – Günter Gaus – to East Berlin in 1974. There were never established formal diplomatic relations between the two German states until the final unification.

The GDR Struggled for Recognition

At the creation of two German states in 1949, the SED continued to hold national reunification as its first priority. In early 1950s, the Soviets did not give up the idea of German unification, nor did their East German comrades. In fact, there has been a widespread Communist optimism that capitalism was on the brink of collapse, and the West German state would not be viable at all.[368] As aforementioned, the year 1955 witnessed two German states respective integration into

---

364 Kilian, 2001: 343–344.
365 Gray, 2003: 211–213.
366 Gray, 2003: 215–217.
367 Gray, 2003: 233.
368 Spilker, 2006: 6.

two conflicting blocs. Only a few days after the FRG's admission into NATO, the Soviet Union and other Eastern European countries found a military alliance on their own, namely the Warsaw Pact. The GDR was a signatory.

Right after Adenauer's leave, Walter Ulbricht and Otto Grotewohl arrived in Moscow. The Soviet Union and the GDR signed the State Treaty in the Kremlin on September 20, 1955, giving full sovereign status to the latter.

In the meanwhile, the GDR was eagerly looking for recognition outside the Soviet bloc. The first target was Finland, who had consular relations with both the FRG and the GDR since 1953 and was viewed by the GDR as the most progressive country in the capitalist world. Concurrently with Ulbricht and Grotewohl, there was a delegation from Finland in Moscow in September 1955. Sponsored by the Soviets, the Finns were prepared to follow the Soviet model to recognize both German states at the same time. The Bonn government reacted quickly and determinedly – instead of dual recognition, it persuaded Finland to continue its policy of non-recognition of divided states. As a result, the Finns stepped back. It was not until 1973 that Finland could finally recognize the FRG and the GDR simultaneously. At the end of the day, Finland turned out to be the only European country that treated both German states equally.[369]

The GDR turned to the South, and reached out those non-aligned. From end of October 1955, a GDR delegation headed by Minister for Foreign Trade and Inter-German Trade Heinrich Rau visited India, where they agreed to relocate the GDR trade mission from Bombay to the capital city, Delhi. The same delegation also visited Egypt and was received by Nasser personally. Egypt and the GDR concluded a three-year trade agreement and agreed to exchange trade representations with consular rights and functions in their respective capitals. These developments were amounted to the imminent possibility of Egypt and India recognizing the GDR.[370] Such a scenario provoked great concerns in Bonn. Fortunately, cautious as Nehru and Nasser, they would not take any further step toward recognition to challenge the FRG position.

The only non-aligned country that formally recognized the GDR was Yugoslavia. Geographically speaking, Tito, as a European, had a stronger motive to take this action than his Asian and African counterparts. And in Berlin, Yugoslavia's recognition was celebrated as an extraordinary diplomatic victory. Obviously, the East Germans hoped that it would trigger a chain reaction

---

369 Hentilä, 2014: 116–130.
370 Winrow, 1990: 38.

among the non-aligned countries. As an anonymous editorial published in *Neues Deutschland* on October 16, 1957 asserted that "the existence of two states in Germany is an indisputable fact. Any government, which actually wishes to safeguard the interests of its own country and those of the peace, will come to the inevitably conclusion from this and normalize their relations with the German Democratic Republic, as was done by the Federal People's Republic of Yugoslavia."[371] The GDR Minister of Foreign Affairs criticized that the FRG's termination of diplomatic relations with Yugoslavia for its recognition of the GDR was a move violating the principles of sovereignty and non-interference, an example of Bonn's imperialist policy.[372]

Encouraged by the breakthrough with Yugoslavia, the MfAA planned to further secure its recognition among the anti-imperialist African and Asian countries, with a special focus on Egypt, Syria, India, Indonesia, and Burma. These targets were carefully picked, for they all faced great economic difficulties at home, which the GDR would have something to offer.[373] As a part of the recognition plan, the GDR granted Egypt two loans. Nasser rewarded in return by first setting up a trade mission in East Berlin in February 1958 and inviting Grotewohl to Cairo in January 1959. During his only visit on the African continent, Grotewohl and Nasser agreed to elevate their trade missions to the status of consulate general. Albeit short of full recognition of the GDR, the FRG retaliated by withdrawing its support for the Aswan Adam.[374] Elsewhere in the Third World East German relations were also slowly opened and consolidated. Until 1961, there were East German consulates in Djakarta and Rangoon. Overall, the GDR lagged behind the FRG in winning diplomatic recognition.

As aforementioned, the FRG impressed the world with its Economic Miracle. Meanwhile, the GDR failed to build a stronger magnet. Worse than that, it experienced economic difficulties at home. The educated and talented East Germans flew into the West, voting with their feet. The GDR failed to build socialism as a model. In the meantime, a nuclear-armed FRG became very likely in the near future. The survivability of the GDR was in question. By the fall of 1958, Khrushchev attempted to involve the West in solidifying the GDR. According to his anticipation, "Western recognition of the SED regime and a reduced or

---

371 *Neues Deutschland*, October 16, 1957, 1.
372 *Neues Deutschland*, October 20, 1957, 1.
373 Kilian, 2001: 33.
374 Winrow, 1990: 54.

eliminated Western presence in West Berlin would significantly alleviate the pressure on East Germany and put it on solid ground."[375]

On November 10, 1958, Khrushchev delivered a speech, claiming that the time had arrived to terminate the remnants of Allied occupation. The Soviet Union would hand over to the GDR the functions in Berlin that were still exercised by the Soviets. If the Western Allies wanted to maintain access to West Berlin, they would have to deal directly with the East Germans.[376] The options offered by the Soviets were quite clear, either granting recognition to the GDR, or giving up West Berlin. This speech triggered one of the most prolonged crises during the Cold War. The West worried that any direct contact with the GDR even at the minimum level would imply recognition of it – precisely what they refused to do ever since the GDR's foundation in 1949. The Eisenhower administration believed that the recognition of the GDR would be a synonym of the allies' failure, which would increase the stability of the Soviet position and encourage a legitimized GDR to become more assertive. On the other side of the Iron Curtain, it would weaken the position of western-oriented politicians like Adenauer and make the West Europeans more insecure.[377] Eisenhower and Dulles would make no concession and showed their willingness to remain in West Berlin even if risking a general war. Khrushchev softened his position and postponed his deadline. He gladly accepted to negotiate with the West in Geneva, and later at Camp David. As noticed by Kitty Newman, the Camp David meeting in September 1959 "saw a sea-change in Eisenhower's attitude to Khrushchev," and it was believed to be "a turning point in East-West relations."[378] At this time the two superpowers were very close to a breakthrough on disarmament and an accommodation on Berlin. Unfortunately, the Paris Summit collapsed after the Soviet Union shot down an American U-2 spy plane on May 1, 1960. Furious and frustrated, however, Khrushchev was still refrained from signing a separate peace treaty with the GDR as he had threatened. Ulbricht grew impatient and sought to deal with the West Berlin issue, instead of waiting for a peace treaty. From September 1960, West Germans were not allowed to enter the GDR

---

375 According to Hope Harrison, Khrushchev's desire to get Western recognition of the GDR, prevent the nuclear arming of West Germany, undermine the Western alliance, and gain strength against his domestic and Chinese critics all contributed to his Berlin Ultimatum. Among them, the top priority was to shore up the GDR. Harrison, 2003: 96.

376 United States Department of States, 1985: 542–546.

377 Burr, 1994: 181.

378 Newman, 2007: 172–173.

territory without a visitor's permit authorized by the GDR Interior Ministry.[379] Step by step, the East Germans seized control over the borders, which eventually ended up in the construction of the Berlin Wall on August 13, 1961. The West powers sent a note to the Soviet Union to protest the erection of the Berlin Wall but made no attempt to crack it down. In fact, this was rather a relief, since "a wall is a hell of a lot better than a war."[380] At the end of the day, the Berlin Crisis proved to be fruitless, with the status of West Berlin unchanged, no peace treaty signed, and the GDR still unrecognized by the West.

According to the GDR official explanation, the closure of borders was a necessary measure to protect its people from West German aggression. However, most of its own people believed that "the border had been closed simply to stop *Republikflucht*."[381] In his famous *Ich bin ein Berliner* speech, Kennedy pronounced the Berlin Wall as "the most obvious and vivid demonstration of the failures of the Communist system."[382] The Wall became a symbol of the inhumanity and repression of the GDR. The closure of boundaries intensified the division of Germany, physically and psychologically alike. The East Germans were walled in the GDR, for whom there was no other way but to orientate themselves to the socialist German state. The Berlin Wall seemed to be the final nail in the coffin of the German reunification. And the GDR lost the moral high ground and could never again claim that it has been working for the reunification.

Alongside the Berlin Crisis was the decolonization. The building of the Berlin Wall damaged the GDR's image in Africa.[383] The GDR also applied *Adressendiplomatie* but failed to secure reciprocate recognition from the newly independent African states.[384] In general, the FRG outperformed the GDR in the Third World. As for the field of diplomatic relations, the FRG hold almost monopoly in the decolonized Africa.

In addition, the GDR failed to obtain any recognition – individual or collective alike – through the Non-Aligned Conference in Belgrade in September 1961. Yugoslavia's recognition in 1957 did not trigger a domino effect among the non-aligned countries as was hoped by the East Germans. And for the Yugoslavs, it was in accordance with non-alignment to recognize the GDR, but then they refused to do anything more than that fearing of weakening their non-aligned

---

379 *Neues Deutschland*, August 31, 1960, 1.
380 Beschloss, 1991: 266.
381 Major, 2010: 123.
382 Kennedy, 1964: 524.
383 Winrow, 1990: 60.
384 Winrow, 1990: 47; Troche, 1996: 29.

position.[385] During the Belgrade Conference, the participating leaders discussed the German question, but opinions varied. In the end, Nehru's view championed. As a result, in the final documents there was no mention of the existence of a second German state.[386] The Belgrade Conference proved that "the Hallstein Doctrine was strong enough to with stand even the most intensive East German diplomatic offensive."[387]

The MfAA complained that its Belgrade legation failed to achieve better – if any – results in Belgrade. Considering that Belgrade was the only capital outside the socialist bloc hosting representatives from East Berlin instead of Bonn, where else could come a breakthrough for the GDR? In hindsight, the answer is nowhere but Bonn.[388]

Since the formation of the Grand Coalition in 1966, Bonn gradually adjusted its approach and moved to normalize its relations with the Soviet states. Inside the East bloc, responses diverged. The East Germans feared of further isolation and bypass, and considered it to be "aggression on slippers."[389] Some Warsaw Pact states were on the verge of normalizing relations with the FRG, for it would increase trade and obtain much-needed hard currency. In an extreme case, the Romanians even expressed a willingness to establish diplomatic relations with Bonn without any preconditions.[390] This raised great alarms in the GDR and Poland. Ulbricht publicly warned the revanchist essence of Kiesinger's policy.[391] Brezhnev voiced support of the GDR on January 13, 1967, declaring that "the unconditional recognition of the GDR as an independent sovereign state is one of the fundamental preconditions for real normalization of situation in Europe."[392] However, the Soviets could hardly block other socialist states from establishing diplomatic relations with Bonn, for Moscow had already done so back in 1955.

On January 31, 1967, Romania established diplomatic relations with the FRG. Facing Bonn's diplomatic offense, the Warsaw Pact member states hold a meeting in Karlovy Vary in February 1967. The GDR proposed that none of the member states should recognize the FRG before the GDR had done so itself, which was later

---

385 Winrow, 1990: 68.
386 Das Gupta, 2014: 152.
387 Maricic, 2019: 142.
388 Cuba recognized the GDR on January 12, 1963, and the FRG broke off diplomatic relations with Cuba two days later. However, Cuba was a socialist country.
389 Niedhart, 2016: 23.
390 Oberländer, 1981: 1293–1297.
391 Oberländer, 1984: 114–124.
392 Oberländer, 1984: 306.

known in the West as the Ulbricht Doctrine.[393] Nonetheless, inside the Soviet bloc, the agreement known as Warsaw Package was reached, which reflected not only thoughts of the East Germans, but also that of the Poles. The secret agreement listed a number of preconditions that Bonn would have to meet before other socialist states would cement diplomatic relations with the FRG, including not only recognition of the GDR, but also recognition of all the existing borders in Europe – the Oder-Neisse Line was specifically mentioned, and renunciation of access to nuclear weapons.[394] Evidently, the East Germans could proclaim the foreign ministers' meeting a success, describing the atmosphere as "comradely cooperation and fully understanding."[395] The East Germans demanded that none of the remaining socialist states establish diplomatic relations with the FRG before the recognition of the GDR was accepted by the FRG first. The unity within the Warsaw Pact preserved for the time being.

In brief, the East Germans were not against the East-West Détente, and only some of them would prefer to seize the initiative and kick off with German-German rapprochement. Unfortunately, the Soviets were always sceptical about a special German-German relationship, and they would rather take the initiative of their own. Consequently, Ulbricht was ousted by Honecker before there were any meaningful achievements from inter-German negotiations.[396] It was only after the Moscow Treaty in 1970 and the Quadripartite Agreement on Berlin in 1971 that Brezhnev gave the go-ahead to Honecker.

As a result, the Basic Treaty was signed on December 21, 1972. The FRG and the GDR formally recognized each other and renounced any attempt to represent the other internationally. This marked the final death of the Hallstein Doctrine. In this December alone, twenty-one states established diplomatic relations with the GDR. And both Germanies were admitted to membership in the United Nations on September 18, 1973. The GDR ultimately came out of diplomatic isolation as the second German state.

Summary

As aforementioned, the division of Germany was not equal. Considering their sizes of area and population, the FRG enjoyed approximately a 3:1 advantage over the

---

393 Staadt, 1993: 232–233.
394 Selvage, 2004: 239.
395 *Neues Deutschland*, February 11, 1967, 1.
396 Grieder, 1998: 14–41; Bange, 2016: 79–81.

GDR, and therefore, to expect that many countries would recognize the FRG solely. However, the FRG was able to achieve a result far better than this. For nearly two decades, Bonn used every method at its disposal to uphold its claim of sole representation. None in the Western bloc recognized the GDR before signing the Basic Treaty. Even European neutral states and the non-aligned African and Asian countries have held the line at Bonn.

The Hallstein Doctrine has been criticized by many politicians and scholars. In his memoir, Grewe complains about the rigidity in implementing it.[397] Kilian argues that the Hallstein Doctrine and the isolation of GDR did not bring the unification of Germany any close.[398] Nevertheless, the Hallstein Doctrine deserves the merits as a successful policy. A quick look at Figure 5-6 will make it clear how successful it is in preventing the recognition of GDR.

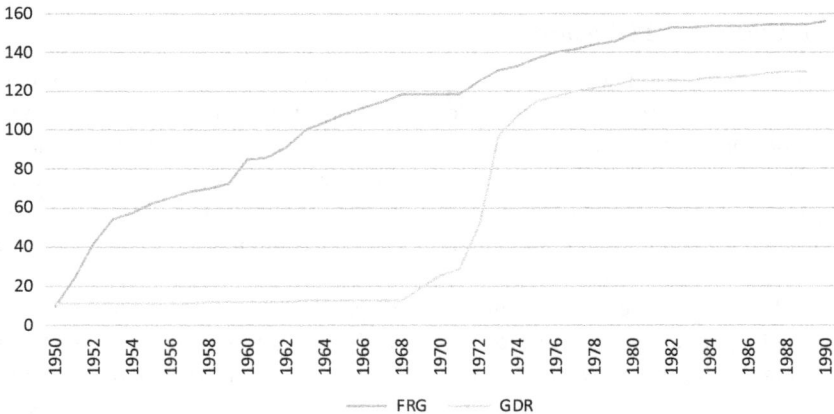

Figure 5-6. Germany: Diplomatic Recognition, 1950–1990

The GDR only secured international recognition at the mercy of four Allies and its arch-rival. It caught up during the 1970s, but still lagged behind the FRG in expanding its diplomatic network world widely. The GDR was both geographically and politically too close to the Soviet Union, which secured its survival for a certain period of time, but also largely restricted its room of manoeuvring. As bluntly pointed out by Helga Hatendorn, "the GDR's existence was defined and

---

397 Grewe, 1979: 253.
398 Kilian, 2001: 377.

justified by its membership in the socialist camp and as an ideological counter-weight to the FRG."[399]

To sum up, the East-West conflict was the dominant effect in the recognition competition between the FRG and the GDR. But we should never overlook the influences of the Germans themselves. The FRG's sole representative claim constantly challenged the GDR's psychological security. To certain point, the GDR's eagerness for recognition was a reflection of its own instability. "Had the legitimacy of the SED been more firmly established within the borders of the GDR," as observed by Mary Elise Sarotte, "the party would not have needed to seek recognition abroad."[400] In hindsight, the GDR failed to develop its own national identity on the social structure to replace German nationalism.

5.3. Korea

The Unexpected Division

Gregory Henderson, a former US diplomat, pointed out in 1974 that "No division of a nation in the present world is so astonishing in its origin as the division of Korea; none is so unrelated to conditions or sentiment within the nation itself at the time the division was effected; none is to this day so unexplained; in none does blunder and planning oversight appear to have played so large a role. Finally, there is no division for which the U.S. government bears so heavy a share of the responsibility as it bears for the division of Korea."[401]

Indeed, the Korean peninsula is a geographically well-defined territory, where its people live in unity for centuries. Korea experienced invasions from its neighboring big powers. As a result of the Sino-Japanese War of 1895 and the Russo-Japanese War of 1904, Japan emerged as the colonial master of Korea, and its occupation lasted until the end of the Second World War. As agreements reached in Cairo, Yalta, and Potsdam, Korea would be free and independent in due course, yet the great powers had no specific arrangement for it.[402] At the eve of Japanese surrender, the Americans hastily proposed to divide the peninsula into two zones of occupation at the thirty-eighth parallel, with Soviet troops occupying the area north of that line, and US troops the area south of it. The

---

399 Haftendorn, 2006: 150.
400 Sarotte, 2001: 170.
401 Henderson, 1974: 43.
402 Kim, 1977: 28–31.

Soviets accepted this proposal with no objections. The Koreans were ignored thoroughly.[403]

In December 1945, Foreign Ministers from the Soviet Union, the United Kingdom, and the United States finally reached an agreement on Korea. The Moscow Agreement was intended to create an independent Korea through a four-power trusteeship, and a Soviet-American Joint Commission was to be established to implement the plan.[404] The Koreans, longing for independence, opposed the trusteeship.[405]

With a deterioration of relations between the Soviet Union and the United States, the Joint Commission failed to produce any progress toward a united, independent Korea. Then the Korean question was transferred to the United Nations, where there was obviously a pro-American majority. The General Assembly adopted a resolution on November 14, 1947 and a Temporary Commission on Korea would be founded to observe elections in Korea for a National Assembly that would establish a Korean government. Despite the Soviet opposition, the UNTCOK began its work in Seoul in January 1948. Since it refused to enter the north, its activities were limited in the south. On February 26, the United Nations adopted an American draft resolution to hold elections in South Korea alone.[406] The resolution met mixed responses in Korea. The advocates of a separate South Korean government enthusiastically supported it, while others criticized it as the perpetuation of the division of Korea, and the communists attacked it and spared no effort to sabotage the proposed elections.[407] Nevertheless, general elections were held in the south on May 10, 1948 under the observation of the UNTCOK.

The National Assembly summoned for the first time on May 31, with a third of its seats left open for future northern representatives. A constitution was adopted on July 12. Syngman Rhee was elected as the first President of the new government on July 20. The Republic of Korea was officially proclaimed on August 15, 1948, and the American military government terminated on the same day. On December 12, 1948, the United Nations General Assembly approved a draft resolution jointly sponsored by Australia, China, and the United States by 48 to 6 with 1 abstention. The resolution declared that "there has been established a lawful government," and stressed that "this is the only such Government

403 Oberdorfer and Carlin, 2013: 5.
404 Sappington, et al., 1967: 820–821.
405 Kim, 1977: 47.
406 The Soviet bloc boycotted the meeting, therefore did not present or cast a vote.
407 Kim, 1977: 62–63.

in Korea."[408] It should be noticed that this resolution was carefully worded to avoid declaring the ROK as the government of the entire Korean peninsula; however, it did not raise any objections to the claim that the ROK is the only legal national government in Korea either. Some observers thus described it as "an international birth certificate."[409] Consequently, this resolution was accepted by the ROK as a support for its claim and became the center pillar of South Korean unification policy.

In the meantime, the General Assembly's resolution on December 12, 1948 was a relief for the Americans. They preferred to recognize the regime in Seoul as the national government of Korea when it was under preparation. They attempted to persuade their friends and allies to take joint action of granting recognition to the ROK, but only the Chinese stood firmly on their side.[410] The United States would not go it alone in extending recognition to the ROK, for such a recognition would fuel the Communist propaganda and revoke dissents among United Nations member states. Nonetheless, the American "special representative" had been working and treated as ambassador in Korea.[411] Citing the resolution on December 12, the United States formally extended full diplomatic recognition to the new government in Seoul on January 1, 1949.[412] The United Kingdom, France, China, and the Philippines followed suit.

In the north, a separate government was under preparation too. As early as November 18, 1947, a committee was set up to draft a provisional constitution. The Supreme People's Assembly was formed. Out of its 572 members, 360 were southern representatives. The constitution was ratified on September 3. The Democratic People's Republic of Korea was proclaimed on September 9, 1948, with Kim Il Sung formally installed as Premier. On September 10, the DPRK required the Soviet Union and the United States to withdraw their troops simultaneously and immediately to pave the way for the unification of Korea. On September 18, the Soviet Union accepted this appeal and announced that its troops would be withdrawn by the end of 1948. On October 12, the Soviet Union recognized the DPRK. Soon the Eastern European countries and Mongolia followed suit. The DPRK applied for membership of the United Nations on February

---

408 United Nations General Assembly, 1948.

409 Briggs, 1950: 170.

410 It was announced on August 12, 1948, the Chinese Government accorded provisional recognition to the Government of Korea and appointed an ambassador to Korea. Reid and Stauffer, 1974: 1272–1273.

411 Reid and Stauffer, 1974: 1290–1292.

412 United States. Department of State, 1949: 59–60.

9, 1949, but this application was not even referred to the Security Council for consideration, as was argued that the General Assembly had already recognized the government of ROK as the only lawful government in Korea.[413]

Table 5-4. Diplomatic Recognition of the ROK/DPRK before the Korean War

States recognized ROK		States recognized DPRK
United States	Soviet Union	Hungary
China, R.	Mongolia	Bulgaria
United Kingdom	Poland	Albania
France	Czechoslovakia	China, PR
Philippines	Yugoslavia	Germany, DR
Spain	Romania	Vietnam, DR

The North Korean regime never abandoned the hope of reunifying the fatherland by force. While encouraging struggle and guerrilla warfare in the South, Kim Il Sung increased the tempo of military build-up in the North. Anticipating the withdrawal of occupation forces, Kim saw a good chance for the military unification of Korea. Furthermore, the American constantly downplayed the strategic importance of Korea no doubt encouraged Kim.[414] With Stalin's blessing, North Korea invaded the South under the slogan of "Fatherland Liberation" on June 25, 1950.

In the absence of the Soviet Union, the Security Council adopted an American-sponsored resolution on June 27, stating that "the Members of the United Nations furnish such assistance to the Republic of Korea as may be necessary to repel armed attack and to restore international peace and security in the area."[415] A United Nations Command under General Douglas MacArthur was set up, with armed forces contributed by sixteen United Nations member states. After a successful landing at Inchon on September 15, 1950, the situation at the battle front shifted in favor of the United Nation forces. They pushed the North Korean forces back quickly, and captured Pyongyang in October. The development not only boosted the South Korean morale, but also kindled their passion for unification by force. Attempting to unify the whole of Korea, the United Nations

---

413 United Nations Security Council, 1949.
414 Glennon, 1976: 79; Reid and Glennon, 1976: 969–978.
415 United Nations Security Council, 1950.The Soviet Union had been boycotting the meeting since January 1950, protesting the presence of the ROC representative.

forces marched farther north rapidly. They were only halted and then rolled back by the Chinese People's Volunteer Army, who crossed the Yalu River and entered the war on October 25. After a series of attacks and counter-attacks, neither side could win a complete victory, and the line of battle stabilized. Negotiations began at Kaesong on July 10, 1951 but turned out to be complicated and unproductive. Thus, the military conflict dragged on for another two years.

The fighting finally stopped with an armistice agreement signed on July 27, 1953. A four-kilometre-wide demilitarized zone was established along cease-fire lines, which were very close to the original thirty-eighth-parallel demarcation line. Technically speaking, the Korean War was never formally ended. Moreover, the hostilities intensified and continued to the present. The once carelessly drawn line became the most militarily fortified border in the world, with the Democratic People's Republic on one side, and the Republic of Korea on the other, facing each other with hatred and suspicion.

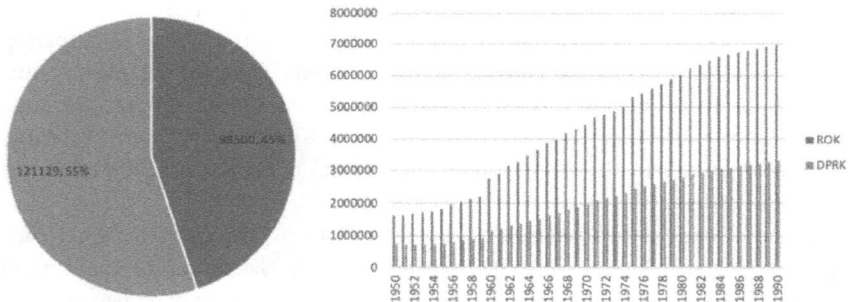

Figure 5-7. Korea: Area and Population

Geographically, the partition of the Korean peninsula seems fairly even. However, the division was not that equal regarding population, as demonstrated in Figure 5-7. No wonder that Pyongyang keeps refusing to hold any kind of nationwide elections suggested by Seoul, since it has a population only half of that of the latter.

What is more, it is important to point out that the two Koreas in the recognition struggle were quite different from what we see currently – as presented in Figure 5-8, the ROK was by no means a highly developed democracy, while the DPRK was somehow projected as a developmental model for recently decolonized countries.

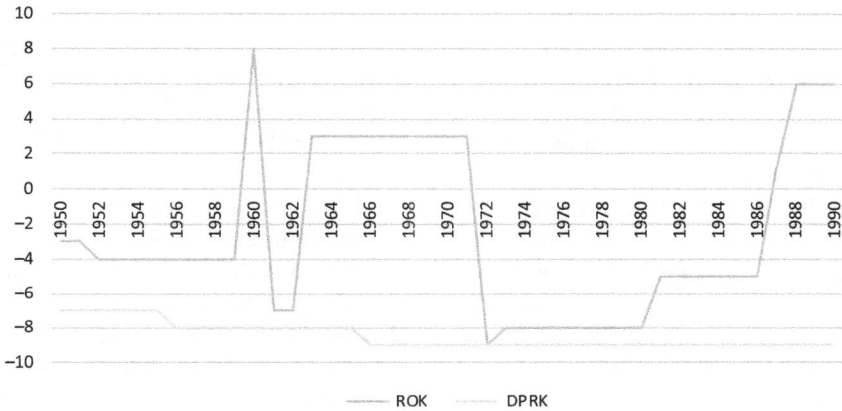

Figure 5-8. Korea: Polity Scores

The DPRK

Ever since its creation, the DPRK had three most important and interrelated goals, namely international recognition, security, and unification.[416] After its failure to achieve unification by force, the DPRK concentrated its efforts on political consolidation and economic reconstruction and adopted the new approach to peaceful unification of Korea. The North Korean policy of peaceful unification was fully developed at the 1954 Geneva Conference. The DPRK Foreign Minister Nam Il proposed that "(1) general elections for a unified All-Korean National Assembly; (2) the organization of an All-Korean Commission, composed of an equal number of representatives from North and South Korea to make the necessary preparations for these elections; (3) urgent measures for the economic and cultural rapprochement of North and South Korea; (4) the withdrawal of all foreign military forces from Korea within six months; and finally (5) a guarantee of the peaceful development of Korea by all those countries most interested in the maintenance of peace in the Far East."[417] While the ROK delegate made a counterproposal that the elections should be based on the principle of proportional representation and conducted under the supervision of the United Nations,[418] the DPRK refused it on the grounds that the United Nations, as a belligerent

---

416 Chung, 1986: 344.
417 United States. Department of State, 1960: 158–159.
418 United States. Department of State, 1960: 176.

party of the war, had lost the moral authority and competence in the settlement of Korean unification. Instead, North Korea proposed a supervisory commission consisting of neutral nations. Nevertheless, the North Korean proposal was unacceptable to the South, and vice versa. The Geneva Conference failed to achieve an agreement on the Korean issue but helped both Koreas develop their respective unification policy.

In October 1954, Kim Il Sung announced that the main task was to build North Korea into a solid democratic base for future unification. He stressed that the unification of Korea could not be achieved without a rapid economic reconstruction and a rise in the living standard of the North Korean people.[419] To this end, a Three-Year Plan for the Rehabilitation and Development of the National Economy was introduced in 1954, and thereafter a Five-Year Economic Plan, which began in 1957 and was accomplished in 1960. Both the Three-Year Plan and the Five-Year Plan were reported successful, and general recovery had been achieved. The Seven-Year Plan launched in 1961 was aimed at full-fledged industrialization. This plan was extended to 1970, as the regime devoted more to increasing defense capabilities, responding to the anti-communist military government in the South. Apparently, the decrease of foreign aid also deepened North Korean difficulties during this period.[420] Regardless of the extraordinary paucity of reliable quantitative data, there was a general agreement that the North Korean economy outperformed that of the South until sometime in the 1970s.[421] One piece of factual evidence was that from December 1959 to December 1961, some eighty-thousand Korean residents in Japan, though mainly originated from the southern part of Korea, voluntarily migrated to the North for repatriation, judging the North to be the better half of the divided peninsula.[422]

While receiving massive aid from fraternal socialist countries, the North Korean leaders carefully distanced the ordinary people from foreigners and downplayed the role of foreign assistance. As early as in December 1955, Kim Il Sung proposed Juche before the KWP propagandists, emphasizing that they would neither follow the Soviet pattern nor copy the Chinese method but to develop a Korean way, taking into account the history, geography, and traditions of their own.[423] As noted by Dae-Sook Suh, Juche "signified the end of political

---

419 Cho, 1967: 225.
420 Armstrong, 2013: 133.
421 Hwang, 1993: 139; Eberstadt, 2010: 33.
422 Wagner, 1961: 132–133.
423 Kim, 1964.

dependence and subservience to the Soviet Union and China."[424] Aware of the economic dependence, Kim promoted Juche to maintain his political and diplomatic independence.

Furthermore, the DPRK managed to exploit the Sino-Soviet rift to its own advantage, extracting assistance while distancing itself from both Beijing and Moscow. In July 1961, Kim Il Sung visited Moscow and signed a Treaty of Friendship, Cooperation, and Mutual Assistance between the USSR and the DPRK. On his way home, Kim signed an almost identical treaty in Beijing. These two alliance treaties solved the North Korean security problem at the time when the Sino-Soviet split was in the open, manifesting Kim's masterful manipulation of Beijing and Moscow.[425]

Entering the 1960s with strength and confidence, Kim Il Sung made a new proposal on unification, calling for the establishment of a Korean confederation to solve the Korean issue by the Koreans themselves without any foreign interference.[426] In addition, he also stressed on cultural and economic exchanges between the two Koreas.[427] The formula of confederation was undoubtedly designed to protect the autonomy of the North Korean government and party, who would be a distinct minority in face of the much more populace South.[428] Thus, Seoul rejected without surprise. As Park Chung Hee came to power in Seoul and lowered the priority of unification, Pyongyang responded by dropping peaceful unification to military self-reliance from 1962.[429]

Nonetheless, it is worth noting that the independent unification plan was more appealing than the unification under supervision proposal, echoing the universal principle of self-determination at that time. These new proposals, along with its economic achievements, impressed not only the Koreans, but also people in the Third World. The DPRK was depicted as "a model of self-reliant development and anti-imperialist independence for the entire Third World."[430] To be sure, independence was the most correct and consistent ideological position that gave Kim Il Sung exclusive right to command nationwide leadership.[431]

---

424 Suh, 1988: 301.
425 Armstrong, 2013: 124–125.
426 The complete withdrawal of the CPVA in 1958 no doubt made Pyongyang's claim to independence more credible. Armstrong, 2013: 107.
427 Cho, 1967: 231–233; Armstrong, 2013: 116.
428 Scalapino, 1963: 35.
429 Do, 2020: 521.
430 Armstrong, 2013: 145.
431 Do, 2020: 528.

Meanwhile, the DRPK expanded its relations with countries in the Third World. The underlying motivations were mainly North Korean self-interest. On the one hand, Kim Il Sung had a good reason to exploit conditions in the Third World to weaken American imperialism. On the other hand, it was important to gain diplomatic recognition as the sole legitimate government of Korea by as many countries as possible.[432] The newly independent African nations were extraordinarily attractive to Pyongyang. The DPRK established diplomatic relations with Algeria and Guinea in 1958, and Mali in 1960.[433] In August 1961, a North Korean goodwill mission was sent to leftist states of West Africa, opening trade and cultural channels with them. The North Korean model of development also appealed to right-wing African leaders.[434] It seemed that there were quite a lot of sympathizers with Juche ideology and admirers of the Great Leader.[435] It is important to note that, in the North Korean view, the admission of newly independent countries into the United Nations would eventually tip the balance of the vote on the Korean issue into its own favor. Such a prediction proved right in the 1970s.

The North Koreans closely followed the rapprochement between the Communist China and the United States, and interpreted it as a signal of American surrender to China. Confident that history was on their side, they initiated direct inter-Korean talks. In August 1971, Kim Il Sung declared that the DPRK was "ready to establish contact at any time with all political parties, including the Democratic Republican Party, and all social organizations and individual personages in South Korea."[436] Though the ROK did not respond officially, a few weeks later the two sides began negotiations first via their respective Red Cross delegations, and then secretly held several rounds of negotiations with high-level intelligence personnel. The result of these talks was a joint declaration on peaceful unification on July 4, 1972.

In its Constitution on 1972, the DPRK for the first time declared Pyongyang as its capital. For a quarter-century, the North Korean government stuck to the narrative that it headed over a unified nation whose capital was Seoul.[437]

---

432 Young, 2015: 100.
433 Wert, et al., 2016: 3.
434 Young, 2015: 101.
435 Park, 2002: 109–110.
436 Oberdorfer and Carlin, 2013: 12.
437 Armstrong, 2013: 137.

However, the relations between Pyongyang and Seoul shifted again to confrontation, along with the renewed American commitment in the South, and the resurgent military build-up in the North.

Along with the dramatic change of the international environment in the early 1970s, Pyongyang made strategic changes in its foreign policy, and began to actively approach capitalist countries. As a result, the DPRK succeeded in establishing diplomatic relations with some European countries, precisely the neutral states.[438] Among the American main allies, Australia was the only country to establish diplomatic relations with the DPRK during the 1970s, while others remained hostile toward the DPRK.

In hindsight, Pyongyang's outward foreign policy proved to be short-lived. Kim Il Sung showed no willingness to make economic reform as that under Deng Xiaoping or what took place in East Europe, thus the DPRK soon retreated even further into self-reliance. Over-reliance on the principle of independence made economic interdependence a horrible idea. Ironically, refused to adjust its economy to an increasingly globalized world, the DPRK suffered economic stagnation and marginalization in the international system.

Nevertheless, the North Korean leaders repetitively stressed that the Korean question must be solved by the Koreans without any external inference, which, as pointed out by Armstrong, "too was a recurrent refrain of the DPRK that would long outlive the Cold War."[439] In other words, the DPRK has been firmly established on nationalism.

The ROK

In contrast to the image today, the ROK took a militant posture and kept reiterating the slogan of "March North and Unify" until the fall of Syngman Rhee in 1960. According to President Rhee, the economy of Korea demanded the unification of the industrial north and the agricultural south. Therefore, the unification should come first, and the sooner, the better. However, unification was an impossible mission, for the ROK only survived on a large amount of American military and economic assistances. Moreover, in Rhee's viewpoint, a war against the North Korean Communists was inevitable a holy war. To him, it was a struggle between life and death, and there could be no coexistence. From Rhee's point of view, even establishing trade relations with the communist regime was

---

438 Choi, 1984: 107–109.
439 Armstrong, 2013: 170.

tantamount to aiding the enemy. Therefore, he regarded the non-aligned policy as a sin, and alienated his country from these countries in Asia and Africa.[440] Although reported to be recognized by some thirty countries, the ROK had been remaining isolated internationally until 1960.[441] In short, the period under Rhee was characterized by ideological confrontation, political repression, economic stagnation (if not recession), social dissatisfaction, and diplomatic isolation. In a stark contrast to the self-reliant DPRK, the ROK appeared to be a black hole of American aids. All these factors led to the revolution in April 1960.

After the election in July 1960, a new government was formed under Premier Chang Myon. The Chang administration abandoned the militant posture of Syngman Rhee, but supported the formula of all-Korea election under the United Nations supervision. More importantly, the new government considered the economic development, instead of unification, to be its top priority.[442] The military revolution in May 1961 brought an end to the Chang administration; however, the inclination to relegate the unification issue to a secondary position in favor of economic construction survived. The military government and the military-turned civilian government under Park Chung Hee took a policy similar to Adenauer's policy of strength, considering the unification of Korea as a goal that could only be achieved by building strength in the South strong enough to prevail the North.[443] In 1962, Park introduced a Five-Year Plan aiming at the industrialization and modernization of the South Korean economy. In contrast to the inward-looking self-reliant economy in the North, the South Korean adopted an export-oriented strategy and took advantage of its educated and disciplined people through the labor-intensive methods of production. The South Korean economy began to grow at a remarkable rate.

At the same time, the ROK moved out from the self-imposed isolation under Syngman Rhee and began to seek wider contacts with the outside world. In general, Park's foreign policy was motivated by the need for economic modernization, maintenance of military preparedness against potential communist invasion, growing nationalism, and the desire to enhance international prestige.[444] The most significant event was the normalization of relations between the ROK and Japan in 1965. The normalization of the ROK-Japan relations made a

---

440 Kim, 1977: 171–172.
441 Clare, et al., 1969: 247.
442 Kim, 1977: 179–181.
443 Lee and Moon, 2020: 182.
444 Clare, et al., 1969: 245.

great contribution to South Korean economic take-off, which brought Japanese compensation and capital investment desperately needed at a time of decline in American aids.[445] Politically, the legitimacy of the ROK was reaffirmed in this bilateral Treaty on Basic Relations, which stated that "the Government of the Republic of Korea is the only lawful Government in Korea as specified in the Resolution 195 (III) of the United Nations General Assembly."[446] The ROK side interpreted this treaty as a bulwark that would prevent Japanese recognition of the other authority.[447]

Park conducted active diplomatic activities and used all the tools available to cultivate friendship around the world. The ROK also continued the practice of its own version of the Hallstein Doctrine, and accordingly suspended its relations with the Republic of Congo and Mauritania in 1964, when these two countries shifted their allegiance to the DPRK.[448] However, the ROK lacked the economic potential to block the DPRK in the way the FRG had done to the GDR.

The ROK assigned much more significance to the United Nations as the primary stage set for its diplomatic competition with the North. As aforementioned, the United Nations resolution of December 12, 1948 had already "placed its stamp of legal validity on the Republic of Korea."[449] Moreover, as a victim of North Korean aggression that was defended by the United Nations, the ROK was in a much-favored position in the community of nations. Even though the ROK could not obtain the membership of the United Nations because of the Soviets' veto power, its representatives could take part in debates over the Korean issues, while the North Koreans were not invited at all. The Soviet bloc and the Western allies were diametrically against each other over issues regarding the United Nations competency and the Korean participation; however, the outcome remained unaffected. The General Assembly, led by a pro-American majority, met no difficulty in passing a pro-ROK resolution each year before 1960.[450] In short, this was a period when the United Nations "was clearly biased toward the ROK."[451] Since 1960, the voting patterns began to change, as more and more countries got tired with the routinized and futile discussions on the Korean issues, and newly admitted members tended to hold a non-aligned position on

445 Gills, 1996: 150.
446 United Nations, 1968: 46.
447 Oda, 1967: 41–42.
448 Gills, 1996: 106.
449 Goodrich, 1956: 69.
450 Kim, 1970: 420–425.
451 Armstrong, 2013: 142.

such a controversial problem. This development was a motivation behind Park's active diplomacy.

Park Chung Hee's rise to power coincided with the escalation of war in Vietnam. As the Johnson administration sought to internationalize the war under the "More Flags" campaign, Park dispatched the ROK troops to Vietnam in 1965. The action was portrayed as a noble defense of freedom against communist aggression, as Park justified his decision: "[w]e cannot sit idly by and assume the attitude of onlooker while our ally falls prey to Communist aggression as if it were a blazing fire on the other bank of the river."[452] Park's commitment to American war effort in Vietnam was not only politically reciprocated by American support for his authoritarian rule at home, but also contributed to the South Korean economic development. As concluded by Charles Armstrong, "the Vietnam War is responsible, in no small measure, for the Korean economic 'miracle' of the 1960s to the 1990s."[453] Domestic discussions about the Vietnam War were silenced by the government; however, the South Korean mercenary participation and their brutal behavior in Vietnam not only fueled Pyongyang's propaganda but also damaged the international image of the ROK. As a result, the ROK had been consistently barred from participating in the conferences of the non-aligned countries.[454]

In late 1960s, echoing the lessening of tensions between the two superpowers, there were growing voices calling for postal, economic, and cultural exchanges between the two Koreas to promote an atmosphere for national unification.[455] For sure, the most significant external change was no doubt the rapprochement between the Communist China and the United States, who once fought directly against each other during the Korean War. At that time, the Koreans worried about being discarded by their respective allies.[456]

At this juncture, the DPRK and the ROK coincidently played the unification card. For the first time since 1953, direct negotiations between the South and the North became possible. Cautiously, the two Koreas conducted talks between the ROK National Red Cross and the DRPK Red Cross Society in August 1971. In parallel to the Red Cross talks were behind-the-scenes high-level secret meetings, resulting in the historic Joint Communique on July 4, 1972. In the Joint Communique,

---

452 Armstrong, 2001: 527.
453 Armstrong, 2001: 531.
454 Lee, 2011: 427.
455 Clare, et al., 1969: 260.
456 Radchenko and Schaefer, 2017: 265; Kim, 2020: 134.

the two sides reached an agreement on principles for unification: "First, unification shall be achieved through independent efforts without being subject to external imposition or interference. Second, unification shall be achieved through peaceful means, and not through the use of force against one another. Third, a great national unity, as a homogeneous people, shall be sought first, transcending differences in ideas, ideologies and systems."[457] It is important to note that unlike the Basic Treaty between the FRG and the GDR, none of the two Koreas' official name was mentioned in this document. This is equal to saying that both Koreas would not recognize one another as a sovereign state.

On June 23, 1973, on the eve of the admission of both German states into the United Nations, Park Chung Hee proposed the entry of both Koreas into that organization; however, he denied that this step would imply the recognition of North Korea as an independent sovereign state. Unlike the German framework of two states in one nation, Park insisted that there was one nation and one state, but two governments. At the same time, he also announced that his government was willing to establish relations with countries that maintained ties with Pyongyang, therefore formally abandoning the South Korean version of Hallstein Doctrine.[458]

Kim Il Sung rejected Park's proposal to join the United Nations on the ground that dual representation in the international body would perpetuate the division of Korea. Moreover, Kim suspended intra-Korean meetings for the same reason.[459] However, Pyongyang sent its delegation to the United Nations as an observer. More than two decades after the United Nations' involvement in the Korean issues, the other side was finally heard at the world forum. As concluded by Chongwook Chung, the DPRK "had attained equal legitimacy at the United Nations."[460] Nevertheless, it would take another two decades for the two Koreas to become official member states of the United Nations.

As it turned out to be, the intra-Korean rapprochement in the early 1970s was short-lived. Concentrating on the diplomatic field, the inter-Korean rivalry moved to a new stage where both Koreas still competed for superiority but no longer objected the de facto coexistence of two Korean states. For most countries

---

457 Ministry of National Unification. Republic of Korea, 1996: 183–184.
458 In practice, ever since 1966 the ROK was aware that it would be necessary to entertain relations with countries that maintained diplomatic ties with the DPRK. What is more, when Chad and the Central Republic of Africa established diplomatic relations with the DPRK in 1969, the ROK did not provoke the Hallstein Doctrine at all. See: Gills, 1996: 165–166; Gu, 1995: 182.
459 Ministry of National Unification. Republic of Korea, 1996: 88.
460 Chung, 1986: 362.

around the world, there was little doubt about the reality that both the ROK and the DPRK were qualified to be accepted as full-fledged members of the international system.[461] By the mid-1970s, Pyongyang caught up and approximately reached parity with Seoul. The resolution of the Korean Question was in impasse.

The changes in international relations and the power configuration in Asia, in particular, offered the South Korean new opportunities. Above all, the establishment of diplomatic relations between Washington and Beijing in 1979, though not wholeheartedly welcomed in Seoul, opened an avenue for its own rapprochement with Beijing. In the 1980s, Seoul continued its diplomatic pragmatism and economic dynamism, clearly exploiting Pyongyang's weakness. Consequently, the ROK diplomacy surged ahead with continuous gains.

The climax was reached at the 1988 Seoul Olympic Games. Despite strong protests from Pyongyang, East European states and China attended the games – considering that the 1980 Moscow and the 1984 Los Angeles Olympics Games were boycotted by the opposing bloc. As illustrated in its motto "Harmony and Progress," the Seoul Olympics were the largest during the Cold War, with representatives from 159 nations from both blocs, a showcase of its economic miracle and a coming-out party for the ROK.[462] Since the next year witnessed a windfall in Europe, it is hard to link directly the Soviet recognition in 1990 and the Chinese move in 1992 to the Seoul in 1988. Nonetheless, it is convinced that the Olympic Games were the "decisive turning point" for improving South Korean relations with the Communist regimes.[463]

Summary

As aforementioned, the relatively even division of the peninsula made neither of the two Korean regimes enjoy an absolute advantage. Following the logic of the Cold War, it is reasonable to expect that the ROK led during the 1950s and 1960s, as shown in the case of China and Germany. However, the ROK under Syngman Rhee was so rigidly anti-communist and so dependent on the United States that it almost isolated itself from the outside world. Only after Park Chung Hee came to the helm did the ROK turn to an outward foreign policy, as reflected in a dramatic growth of diplomatic recognition in the early 1960s. In the meantime, the DPRK actively pursued friendship from the Third World. In the late 1960s, Kim Il Sung successfully made himself a great leader in nationalist and anti-imperialist

---

461 Clough, 1987: 275.
462 Bridges, 2008: 1939.
463 Gills, 1996: 225.

terms. The breakthrough only came in the early 1970s, as the two Koreas no longer opposed recognition of each other. Nevertheless, they have never recognized each other. In the 1980s, while the ROK continued to expand in diplomacy, the DPRK retreated into self-isolation; therefore, the gap expanded once again, as clearly shown in Figure 5-9. Before the end of the Cold War, Pyongyang's allies had already begun to approach Seoul. And the North Korean were informed that none of their allies would cast a veto if the ROK applied for the UN membership. Fearing of total desertion, the DPRK reluctantly joined the international body along with the ROK on September 17, 1991.[464] As a matter of fact, the cross-recognition in the early 1990s did not end up in the equal recognition of the DPRK and the ROK.

As a Korean speaking of being a shrimp between whales, and when the whales fight, the shrimp suffers; the Korean people have been sensitive to its external circumstances.[465] Thus, it could be concluded that the international environment influenced the diplomatic recognition of the two Koreas. By and large, the two superpowers encountered no difficulty in holding their respective allies from stepping out of line.

Nevertheless, how the Koreans responded to the outside changes also mattered significantly. Gills argues that "the role of adaptation to international trends is paramount in explaining success and failure in diplomacy."[466] How they would react could be predicted. Since the 1960s, the rivalry has been settled in a case of State Capitalism versus Juche.[467] Therefore, unless it could develop a new set of identities, Pyongyang could never embrace reforms and openness. Guiding by Juche, the DPRK is not likely to give in to any foreign pressure, and might have to endure diplomatic isolation for a prolonged period.

464 Armstrong, 2013: 280–281.
465 Olsen, 2005: 4.
466 Gills, 1996: 257.
467 Park, 2002: 121.

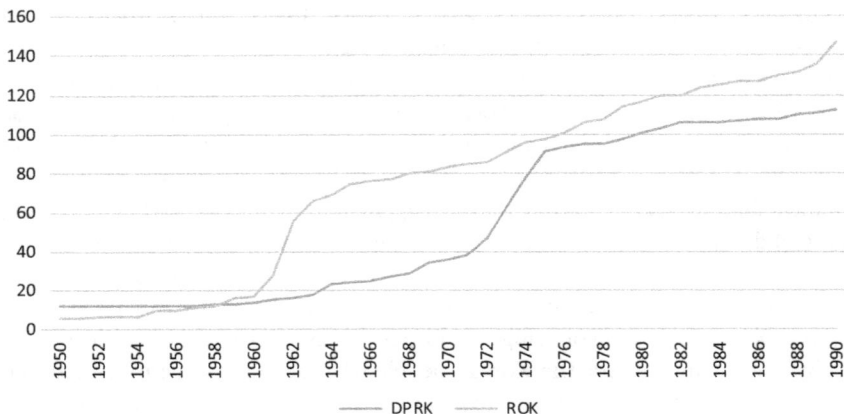

Figure 5-9. Korea: Diplomatic Recognition, 1950–1990

5.4. Vietnam

Division from Potsdam to Geneva

During the Second World War, the Japanese ousted the French, and coerced Bao Dai, the last emperor of the Nguyen dynasty, into declaring the Empire of Viet-Nam to be "independent" from France and become a member of "Greater East Asia Co-Prosperity Sphere." After the Japanese capitulation, Vietnam fell into a dual division. According to the allies' agreement reached previously at the Potsdam Conference, Indochina would be divided at the sixteenth parallel – the Chinese would take the north, and the British the south. Although sympathetic with the Vietnamese people's desire for independence, the Chinese nationalists did not dare to irritate their French ally. In early 1946, the Chinese and French reached an agreement in Chongqing: the French gave up all the privileges in China, and Chinese forces would retreat from Vietnam in return.[468] In the south, the British forces came almost hand in hand with the French and helped restore the French colonial rule.

In the meanwhile, Bao Dai abdicated on August 25, 1945, and handed power over to the Viet Minh. The Viet Minh was greatly reinforced, since Bao Dai's gesture conferred the "mandate of heaven" on Ho Chi Minh, giving the latter

---

468 Yang, 2011: 26.

the legitimacy that had traditionally resided in the emperors.[469] On September 2, Ho declared the independence of his country, and issued the *Declaration of Independence of the Democratic Republic of Vietnam*. As his Declaration began with a quotation from the *United States Declaration of Independence*, Ho also looked upon the United States for support. However, unlike the friendly and cooperative OSS staff in the field, politicians in Washington were indifferent at best, if not hostile to the development in Indochina. All the telegrams Ho wired fell on deaf ears. The self-determination of Vietnamese people had to wait to be determined.

The French were coming back quickly. On September 23, French forces overthrew the local government of the DRV in Saigon, and gradually retook control from south to north. Through the autumn and winter of 1945–1946, Ho Chi Minh sent a series of requests to the United States asking for intervention, but none of them was answered.[470] Under great military pressure, Ho agreed to negotiate with the French over the future status of Vietnam. They signed an accord on March 6, 1946, in which the French recognized the DRV as a free state within the Indochinese Federation and the French Union. However, this accord has never been ratified by Paris. A full-scale war between the French and the Viet Minh broke out in December 1946. The French dominated the cities, albeit they were unable to eliminate the Viet Minh forces. The war became a stalemate.

From 1945 to 1949, the DRV was in total isolation, both geographically and diplomatically. It applied for UN membership in vain for the first time on November 22, 1948. The Vietnamese communists had made repeated efforts to forge contacts with the Soviet Union, but all came to naught.[471] The landscape was then altered, as the victory of Chinese Communist Party brought a strong support to the Viet Minh and bridged the latter's way to the communist community.

The Vietnamese paid close attention to the situation in China. Ho Chi Minh sent Mao Zedong a congratulatory letter on December 5, 1949 and visited China personally on January 2, 1950.[472] In Ho's talks with the Chinese leaders, mutual

---

469 Karnow, 1984: 146.
470 United States. Department of Defense, 1971: I.A. 24.
471 Stalin's aloofness toward Vietnam has been the subject of many scholars, such as Goscha, 2006; Olsen, 2007; Vu, 2009; Szalontai, 2018.
472 The DRV came much later than other communist countries in recognizing the PRC. Ho Chi Minh took a cautious policy, and this delay was thought to be influenced by the very fact that some southern provinces in China were still under the control of the KMT forces at that time. See Chen, 1969: 228–229.

recognition was agreed upon, and substantial assistance was assured.[473] Following the suggestion from Chinese comrades, on January 14, 1950, Ho Chi Minh published a declaration to the governments of the countries all over the world, announcing that the government of the Democratic Republic of Vietnam "is the only lawful government of the entire Vietnamese people. On the basis of common interests, it is ready to establish diplomatic relations with the Governments of all countries which respect the equality, territorial sovereignty and national independence of Viet Nam in order to contribute to safeguarding peace and building world democracy."[474] And the next day, the DRV Foreign Minister Hoang Minh Giam telegrammed his Chinese counterpart Zhou Enlai: "The government and people of the Democratic Republic of Vietnam … announced the recognition of the government of the People's Republic of China under the Chairman Mao Zedong. In order to promote the friendship and cooperation between the Chinese and Vietnamese peoples, the government of the Democratic Republic of Vietnam decided to establish formal diplomatic relations with the government of the People's Republic of China and exchange ambassadors."[475] Zhou responded on January 18.[476] This is the greatest breakthrough the DRV had ever made since its establishment, which, according to Christopher Goscha, "saved the DRV from what might well have been devastating national and international marginalization at a crucial juncture in the battle to keep the DRV alive."[477]

What is more, the Chinese leaders further suggested the Soviets recognizing the DRV, and invited Ho Chi Minh to Moscow to talk to Stalin directly.[478] The recognition of the DRV had been thoroughly discussed between Stalin and Mao. The Soviet leader agreed to follow the Chinese lead; however, afraid of alienating the French, he hesitated to announce it. It was the French National Assembly's ratification of the Elysée Accords on January 29 that helped Stalin make up his mind in recognizing the DRV.[479] The Soviet Union recognized the DRV on January 30, and the official statement was released the following day.[480]

---

473 Luu, 2000: 96.
474 Ho, 1961: 191–192.
475 Archives of the Ministry of Foreign Affairs, 2006b: 245.
476 The DRV made this date a commemoration day. See Chen, 1969: 254–256.
477 Goscha, 2009: 210.
478 Ho Chi Minh visited the Soviet Union in secret on February 3, 1950. See Luu, 2000: 97.
479 Szalontai, 2018. The Elysée Accords were signed between the French President Vincent Auriol and the Vietnamese Chief of State Bao Dai on March 8, 1949, which promised to grant independence to the State of Vietnam.
480 The exchange of diplomatic representatives came much later. The first Vietnamese ambassador to the Soviet Union, Nguyen Long Bang, arrived in Moscow in April 1952.

Did Stalin's recognition reveal the true color of Ho Chi Minh in the way the US Secretary of State Acheson claimed?[481] Definitely, the assumption that the Viet Minh was a part of the international communist conspiracy was the cornerstone of the US involvement in Indochina. Nevertheless, compared to the support offered to the Indonesian, the Soviet Union could have recognized the DRV much earlier. In reality, Stalin was quite indifferent to Vietnam. Stalin's strategy had always been Europe-centric, and the Indochina problem was left to the French Communist Party at large. What is more, he never trusted the Vietnamese leaders. The dissolution of the Indochinese Communist Party in November 1945 further increased doubts about Ho Chi Minh's internationalist communist fiber.[482] There were three main factors leading to the change in Stalin's attitude in 1950: first, the CCP's march to the south made Vietnam geographically accessible; second, the relation between the Soviet and the French worsened significantly with the creation of the NATO; third, the Bao Dai solution would provide an alternative, which was a scenario considered unacceptable to Stalin.[483] Four and half years after its founding, the DRV was finally recognized by the strongest communist power.

Table 5-5. Communist Bloc's Recognition of the DRV

Country	Date
China, PR	1950.01.18
Soviet Union	1950.01.30
Korea, DPR	1950.01.31
Czechoslovakia	1950.02.02
Hungary	1950.02.03
Romania	1950.02.03
Germany, DR	1950.02.03
Poland	1950.02.04
Bulgaria	1950.02.08
Albania	1950.02.11

The first Soviet ambassador to the DRV, Aleksandr Andreevich Lavrishchev, arrived in Hanoi in September 1954.

481 Petersen, et al., 1976: 711.
482 Goscha, 2006: 59–103.
483 Szalontai, 2018: 3–56.

Within a month, as listed in Table 5-5, North Korea and Eastern European communist countries followed suit.[484] The DRV thus officially sided with the communist bloc. After failing to obtain support from the West, and then the neighboring Asian countries, the Vietnamese got aids they desperately needed from the Soviet and Chinese communists at last. They cheered, "and then volunteered to fight on the frontlines" of the Cold War.[485] The war moved beyond the Vietnam-France framework, and developed into a Cold War conflict.

In order to undermine the DRV's influence and legitimacy and make the war look less colonial, the French welcomed the return of the former emperor Bao Dai as the Chief of State of a new Vietnamese authority. The State of Vietnam was officially established on July 2, 1949. However, the French granted Vietnam only limited autonomy. As some observed, "no actual transfer of political power occurred."[486] Therefore, even though it was widely believed that recognition by Western powers and commonwealth nations would rally the Vietnamese nationalist support of Bao Dai instead of Ho Chi Minh, the United States and the United Kingdom were refrained from an early recognition of the SVN.[487] This implied the fundamental difference between France and its allies: The Bao Dai solution was initiated by the French as a means to maintain its control and justify its war effort, while the American and British saw it as a means to achieve an independent Vietnamese state.

Time was running short. Before the French were forced to accord full independence to the Vietnamese people, Chinese and Soviet recognition of the Democratic Republic of Vietnam in January 1950 signaled the arrival of the Cold War at Indochina. Following the Cold War logic, the United States had no other choice but to throw its weight behind France. On February 7, 1950, only one week after the Soviet's recognition of the DRV, the United States recognized the State of Vietnam as an independent state within the French Union. The United Kingdom also recognized SVN on the same day, but in a more realistic way to describe the SVN as "an associated state" within that Union.[488] And as the war broke out in the Korean peninsula, French, American and British diplomats doubled their efforts to persuade or press the "free world" and non-communist

---

484 It should be noted that except the PRC, none had sent a diplomatic mission to the DRV until the conclusion of the Geneva Conference.
485 Vu, 2009: 173.
486 United States. Department of Defense, 1971: I.A. 40; Petersen, et al., 1976: 704–711.
487 Reid, 1975: 33–38.
488 Foreign Office, 1965: 65.

states to recognize the Bao Dai regime and head off the "red tide." By the end of 1950, eighteen states had recognized the State of Vietnam.[489]

However, this did not change the fact that the State of Vietnam associated with the French Union was little more than a façade held up by the French colonialism. Newly independent Asian countries were extremely sensitive on this issue. For nationalist leaders across the region, their overarching task was not anti-communism but decolonization. Nonetheless, the importance of anti-colonialism was largely underestimated by the Western powers. The more the West pressed on the recognition of the SVN, the less likely the Asian would do so. Nehru made it fairly clear that India would not recognize Bao Dai regime because the latter "suffered from this leader's past record and was still too much under French tutelage."[490] As the US ambassador in Thailand reported, "It is transparently clear that Asiatic neighbors of Indochina consider Bao Dai a French creation and a French puppet; despite current and anticipated actions of support by US and western powers they prepared [sic] sell his regime short, if status Bao Dai remains undrastically modified [sic]; even if such changes made promptly, he must exert effective leadership comparable to Ho's."[491] The former colonial master was reluctant to make further concessions to grant complete independence to Vietnam until it was too late.

With the end of diplomatic isolation, economic and military assistance flew in, which helped reverse the tide on the battlefield. The military situation was transformed from small-scale guerrilla operations to a war of movement. In March 1954, the Viet Minh launched the battle of Dien Bien Phu, and decisively defeated the French forces in May. The defeat seriously weakened the French position in Geneva, where the future of Indochina would be negotiated.

The second phase of the Geneva Conference, from May 8 to July 21, 1954, was participated in by the United States, France, the United Kingdom, the Soviet Union, the People's Republic of China, Cambodia, Laos, the State of Vietnam, and the Democratic Republic of Vietnam. During preparations for the conference, the French policy concerning the so-called "interested states" was not identical with that of the US. The French pressured to exclude the Indochinese from

---

489 They were Australia, Belgium, Brazil, Chile, Colombia, Cuba, Greece, Italy, Luxembourg, the Netherlands, New Zealand, South Africa, South Korea, Spain, Thailand, the Vatican, the United Kingdom, and the United States. See Colbert, 1977: 209.

490 *The Times*, January 13, 1950, 4.

491 Petersen, et al., 1976: 739.

the Geneva Conference, which, according to McClintock, then the US Chargé at Saigon, "is foolish and will merely serve to confirm suspicions here and elsewhere in Asia that Associated States are not in fact independent." [492] No matter how it was grudging to seat and negotiate with the Viet Minh, the US viewed the absence of the Associated States as undesirable. Bao Dai and Buu Loc were so deeply disturbed by the prospect of facing the Viet Minh as a full participant across the conference.[493] However, they could not afford to be accused of sabotaging an international effort to end the war. Besides, it was also hoped that discussions at Geneva would induce non-communists of Viet Minh to break away from Ho Chi Minh.[494] On accepting the invitation, Bao Dai's Foreign Minister Nguyen Quoc Dinh made three conditions: firstly, he opposed any proposal against the territorial integrity and political unity of Vietnam; secondly, the presence of the Viet Minh should not be interpreted as recognition of it as a state; thirdly, some actions should be taken to evacuate the wounded in Dien Bien Phu.[495] The nine-participator list was settled only on May 4, shortly before the opening of the Indochina phase of the conference.

Even though seating at the same conference table for the first time, two Vietnams were treated differently. As the negotiation went on, the importance of the DRV position gradually increased, since the primary issue of this conference was to make an armistice between the French and the Viet Minh. While the French and other chief delegates of the great powers negotiated directly with Pham Van Dong, Bao Dai's delegates were largely ignored.

On July 21, 1954, the Geneva Accord was signed.[496] Accordingly, a provisional military demarcation line should be drawn at the seventeenth parallel; an International Commission for Supervision and Control composed of representatives from Canada, India and Poland should be set up to ensure the execution of the agreement; and general elections should be held in July 1956 to bring about the unification of Vietnam.

The Geneva Conference marked the end of the French war in a temporary division of Vietnam. There was a widespread consensus that the partition was forced upon the Vietnamese under great pressure, if not by betrayal, of the Soviet and the Chinese. As Chen and Shen wrote bluntly, "the young

---

492 Kitchens and Petersen, 1981: 432.
493 Kitchens and Petersen, 1981: 515–516.
494 Kitchens and Petersen, 1981: 666.
495 Kitchens and Petersen, 1981: 669–670.
496 However, the date signed was July 20, 1954, in order to meet the deadline that was set by the French Prime Minister Mendes-France.

Vietnamese communists had no other choice but to follow Beijing's and Moscow's advice to accept a peace accord that would divide Vietnam – albeit temporarily, it was intended – along the seventeenth parallel."[497] However, this "standard total view" overlooked Vietnamese motivations.[498] The Viet Minh had its own interests in achieving a negotiated solution: First of all, according to their calculation, the balance of forces in Indochina was not in their favor. Even though the Battle of Dien Bien Phu was a glorious victory, the Vietnamese had not gotten the crucial threshold necessary to impose an overwhelming victory in all of Vietnam. The French Union forces, with the backing of the United States, were still much more advantageous than the Viet Minh forces, both in quantity and in quality. Second, the Viet Minh was feared of a direct US military intervention, which might postpone their victory indefinitely. At the time, the Americans were already considered as the DRV's "Enemy No. 1." The Vietnamese communists worried over the nationalist character of Ngo Dinh Diem government, and considered that Diem was backed by the US, whose appointment was the first step of the Americans to replace the French and intervene in Indochina.[499] Furthermore, the escalation of war would inevitably expand the involvement of its communist allies. Even if not direct military intervention, large-scale aid could also become dangerous, restraining the Viet Minh's freedom of action and nationalist appeal. Last, but not least, the Viet Minh also needed a peaceful environment to consolidate its own power and rebuild its war-torn economy.[500] Overall Ho Chi Minh described the Geneva Conference as a great victory.[501]

---

497 Chen and Shen, 2008: 8.
498 According to Tao Wang, the relations among the PRC, the DRV and the Soviet Union were cooperative and coordinated. They all accepted the necessity to negotiate a cease-fire in Indochina to avoid potential American intervention; their primary difference was how and where to draw the line of demarcation. See Wang, 2017: 3–42.
499 Kitchens and Petersen, 1981: 1347. In replacement of Buu Loc, Ngo Dinh Diem became the SVN prime minister and established his cabinet on July 7, 1954.
500 Asselin, 2013: 11–43; Goscha, 2017: 287–294.
501 Ho, 1962: 17–20.

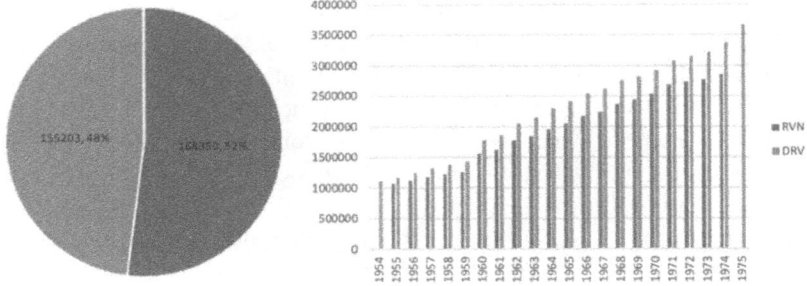

Figure 5-10. Vietnam: Area and Population

As a result of multilateral negotiations, Vietnam turned out to be more evenly divided than other three nations, both in terms of area and population, as presented in Figure 5-10.

The most significant distinction between the two parts was that the Viet Minh had fought the French forces, and for this reason, the DRV "possessed credibility as defenders of the nation that no American money or arms could buy for its clients."[502] Recognizing its disadvantages in anti-colonialism, the South Vietnamese regime, along with their American patrons, beautified itself through democratic elections. The RVN had a much higher polity score than its counterparts, as shown in Figure 5-11.

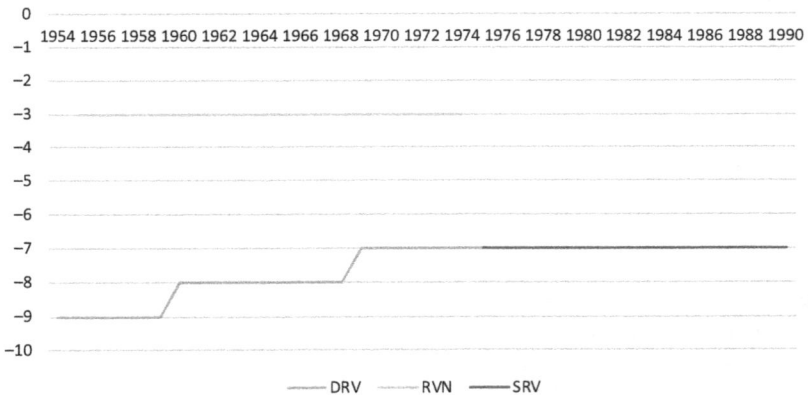

Figure 5-11. Vietnam: Polity Scores

---

502 Gilbert, 2002: 14.

The RVN

While participating in Geneva, the SVN government was on the edge of collapse at home. By filling the government with his family and loyalists and using forces to crack the sects down, Ngo Dinh Diem consolidated his power, and eventually convinced the Americans of his ability to bring stability to the south half of Vietnam.

The State of Vietnam and the United States did not sign the agreements. In the close secession of the Geneva Conference, the SVN Foreign Minister Tran Van Do protested vehemently against the partition of Vietnam. In a clear contrast with the Viet Minh's willingness to sell out the territorial integrity of the fatherland, such a psychological move was expected to evoke favorable response from Vietnamese people and attract popular support for the newly formed government under Ngo Dinh Diem. Across the Atlantic Ocean, at his news conference on the same day, President Eisenhower commented frankly that the agreement contained features that they did not like, and announced that "the United States has not itself been party to or bound by the decisions taken by the Conference."[503] Peace and unification were shadowed.

Ngo Dinh Diem and his supporters sketched out a distinctive brand of Vietnamese nationalism, according to which the Vietnamese nation faced three enemies – feudalism, colonialism, and communism.[504] On July 20, 1955, the first anniversary of the Geneva Accords, Diem launched the Denounce the Communist Campaign, through which the Saigon government and its allied intellectuals created a new political vocabulary that described Vietnamese nationalism and communism as not only mutually exclusive but entirely opposite to each other. According to the dichotomy of "Quoc gia" (country) and "Viet Cong" (Vietnamese Communism), the DRV was depicted as "a traitor to the anticolonial resistance, a servant of international communism, and an oppressive regime."[505]

As a former emperor and a French puppet, Bao Dai was the most imminent icon of both feudalism and colonialism, who must be ousted. Ngo Dinh Diem overthrew Bao Dai in the plebiscite of October 23, 1955, with 98.2 % of the votes. Regardless of numerous discussions about its undemocratic nature, the referendum was carefully structured as a choice for or against an unpopular former emperor, and closely linked to the popular concept of republicanism, which

---

503 Kitchens and Petersen, 1981: 1503.
504 Miller, 2013: 129–136.
505 Tran, 2013: 24.

ensured an overwhelmingly favorable response.[506] Long before the referendum, the Americans had already recognized that it would be not possible for Bao Dai to establish an adequate control, let alone compete against Ho Chi Minh for the allegiance of the Vietnamese people in a coming nation-wide election, if there would be any.[507] The oust of an unwelcomed ex-emperor was no big deal at all. The American officials were more concerned with how the plebiscite would be viewed internationally, and they tried their best to portrayed it as a democratic practice taking place in a former colonized state, a self-determination of the Vietnamese people to welcome the progressive republicanism, and the first stage of the political transformation to build Vietnam into a stronghold of the free world.[508]

On October 26, when the result of the Diem-Bao Dai referendum was announced, Diem proclaimed the founding of the Republic of Vietnam and declared himself the President. No matter how reluctant to jettison Bao Dai, the French recognized the RVN immediately.

By the second anniversary of the Geneva Accords, Ngo Dinh Diem had made himself "the uncontested ruler of the RVN."[509] John F. Kennedy highly praised Diem's impressive achievements:

"...Most striking of all, perhaps, has been the rehabilitation of more than 3/4 of a million refugees from the North. For these courageous people dedicated to the free way of life, approximately 45,000 houses have been constructed, 2,500 wells dug, 100 schools established, and dozens of medical centers and maternity homes provided.

"Equally impressive has been the increased solidarity and stability of the Government, the elimination of rebellious sects and the taking of the first vital steps toward true democracy. Where once colonialism and Communism struggled for supremacy, a free and independent republic has been proclaimed, recognized by over 40 countries of the free world. Where once a playboy emperor ruled from a distant shore, a constituent assembly has been elected."[510]

The Hanoi regime expected to win the unification of Vietnam through the general elections promised by the Geneva Accords; however, the Saigon regime insisted that the Republic of Vietnam was never a signatory of the agreement and, therefore, was not bound by it at all. In a statement broadcasted on July 16, 1956, Ngo Dinh Diem emphasized that:

506 Miller, 2004: 208.
507 Kitchens and Petersen, 1981: 437–464.
508 Keefer and Mabon, 1985: 589–595; Chapman, 2006: 676.
509 Tran, 2013: 69.
510 Kennedy, 1956.

"...no maneuver from whatever origin shall divert us from our goal, the unity of our country, but a unity in freedom and not in slavery.

"We do not reject the principle of elections as peaceful and democratic means appropriate to achieving this unity. However, if elections constitute one of the bases of true democracy, they shall have their 'raison d'être' only on the condition of being absolutely free.

"Now, faced with the regime of oppression as practiced by the Communists in North Vietnam, we remain skeptical as to the possibility of achieving the conditions for a free election in the North."[511]

Table 5-6. Diplomatic Recognition of the DRV/RVN by July 1956

DRV		RVN		
China, PR	United States	Philippines	Argentina	Honduras
Soviet Union	France	Spain	Costa Rica	Colombia
Korea, DPR	United	Cuba	Canada	Sudan
Czechoslovakia	Kingdom	Haiti	Laos	Jordan
Germany, DR	Australia	Bolivia	Turkey	Portugal
Hungary	New Zealand	Equateur	Belgium	
Romania	Thailand	Brazil	Austria	
Poland	Japan	Liberia	Germany, FR.	
Bulgaria	Italy	Nicaragua	Vatican	
Albania	China, R.	Chile	South Africa	
Mongolia	Korea, R.	Greece	Guatemala	
Indonesia	Netherlands	Luxembourg	Venezuela	

July 1956 passed in silence. The general elections called for by the Geneva Agreements had never been held. And it was clear to all concerned parties that there would be no general elections in the foreseeable future. Consequently, the provisional demarcation line between the Viet Minh and the French forces became a permanent territorial boundary between the Democratic Republic of Vietnam and the Republic of Vietnam, with both of them recognized by several countries respectively, as listed in Table 5-6.

As the president of the RVN, Ngo Dinh Diem was determined to build his nation different than that of Ho Chi Minh. Struggling to survive in the Cold War, Diem's foreign policy was built on the close alliance with the free world, among which the United States was no doubt the most significant. In his 21-day state visit to the United States in May 1957, Diem described what he achieved in Vietnam as a pilot experiment, which showed the others what the good American aid can bring.[512] As noticed by Henderson and Fishel, "Diem approached the conduct of

---

511 Vietnam National Archives Center II, 1961.
512 Keefer and Mabon, 1985: 796–797.

foreign policy armed with certain basic preconceptions. Perhaps most important were his convictions as to the necessity, on grounds of realpolitik, for smaller countries to align themselves unequivocally in the cold war; and as to the immorality of nonalignment."[513]

Small and weak, the RVN relied upon the US and its allies to boost its own international prestige. Thailand was the best friend and the very first Asian state to recognize the RVN. In West Asia, it could count on Turkey. Though geographically apart, many European and Latin American states established diplomatic relations with Diem's regime as well. Relations with the West were mainly coordinated in Washington, Paris, and London, later also in Bonn. With always limited budgets, it was totally understandable that diplomats were simultaneously accredited to more than one capital.

Nonetheless, it is too exaggerated to label Diem's policy nothing but anti-communist. Rather than merely following the American instructions, as blamed by the DRV, Diem was determined to pursue an independent foreign policy of his own. On the one hand, the RVN's relations with other anti-communist regimes were not determined simply by concerns about containing communism. Having a close look at the RVN-ROC relations can illustrate this easily. Jiang Jieshi should be Diem's best friend, for they were geographically, culturally and ideologically close to each other, and more importantly, they both had an incomplete enterprise of reuniting their countries while facing strong rival communist regimes. Conversely, the relations between them were only elevated to the ambassadorial level in 1957, after Diem modified his policy towards the Chinese minority in Vietnam. Even with development, the friendship between Diem and Jiang was never as cordial as that between Ho and Mao.[514] Another example was Diem's apparently lack of interest in forming close relations with Pakistan. Although the diplomatic relations were established on November 11, 1957, Diem did not send any representative to Karachi, and he never visited Pakistan.

On the other hand, Diem's attitude towards non-aligned countries was not so inflexible and hostile as some historians have criticized.[515] As early as 1955, by accepting invitation to the Afro-Asian Conference, Diem was determined to cultivate and maintain friendly relations with neutralist countries. He was of the conviction that instead of the confrontation between the East and the West, "the real problem of the countries that met at Bandung is the problem

---

513 Henderson and Fishel, 1966: 7.
514 Lim, 2014.
515 Such as critics in Henderson and Fishel, 1966.

of underdevelopment."[516] Diem thought highly of the conference; if not for the domestic political crisis, he would have been in Bandung personally.[517] As the most prominent advocate of neutralism, Indian Prime Minister Jawaharlal Nehru refused to recognize either of the two Vietnams, but attempted to remain friendly with both sides – India maintained consulate level relations with both the North and the South.[518] No matter how harshly he criticized Nehru behind the scene, especially in private with his younger brother and political advisor Ngo Dinh Nhu, Diem was restrained in his dealings with the Indian leader. In November 1957, during his official visit to Delhi, Diem exalted Nehru's role in promoting India's independence, and praised India's contribution through the work of the International Commission toward maintaining peace in Southeast Asia.[519]

Being aware of the decolonizing tide, the RVN identified itself as a newly independent state freed from the yoke of French colonialism, therefore a member of the Third World. Sharing the bitter colonial experience, Diem cultivated friendly relations with the emerging states of Asia and Africa. Having an embassy in Paris brought great convenience on building connections with those new states in West Africa. Vietnamese diplomats closely followed the decolonizing negotiations, and would send letters to grant official recognition to new governments as soon as the independence was clear. This strategy was extremely successful: the RVN established diplomatic relations with Cameron, Cote d'Ivoire, Dahomey, Madagascar, Morocco, Niger, Nigeria, Republic of Congo, Senegal, Togo, Tunisia, and Upper Volta respectively. Moreover, Diem paid considerable attention to the events on that continent by sending observers to various kinds of gatherings.

Consistently refusing to have any form of relations with any communist regime, Ngo Dinh Diem never refrained from showing antagonism to the states that moved close to the communists. In 1960, when Mali was on the eve of independence, its leaders announced its willingness to establish friendship with all

---

516 Keefer and Mabon, 1985: 100.

517 An eleven-member delegation from the State of Vietnam was headed by the Minister of Planning and Reconstruction Nguyen Van Thoai. Vu Van Mau, President of the Court of Appeal at that time, also attended. Meanwhile, that of the DRV was consisted of sixteen delegates, mainly the officials from the Ministry of Foreign Affairs, leaded by its Deputy Prime Minister and Minister for Foreign Office Pham Van Dong. See: Centre for the Study of Asian-African Developing Countries, 1983: 206–207.

518 On January 7, 1972, India established full diplomatic relations at the ambassadorial level with the North.

519 Thien, 1963: 138.

the countries. Such an attitude raised concerns in Saigon, and Foreign Minister Vu Van Mau even urged to send a delegation to Bamako before the independent ceremony to prevent Mali from recognizing the DRV. However, when it became clear that Mali would establish diplomatic relations with Hanoi, Diem cut all the contacts, and mentioned no more relations with Mali.[520]

Things were more troubling in the case of Laos. Diplomatic relations were built between Saigon and Vientiane in 1956. Bordering both the DRV and RVN, Laos was viewed as an infiltration route used by the communists. The 1961 Geneva Conference on Laos formally declared the neutrality of Laos, and created a coalition government composed of communist, anti-communist and neutralist forces. But it made no attempts to cut off the Ho Chi Minh Trail. What is worse, the coalition government decided to exchange ambassador with Hanoi in 1962. Vu Van Mau sent a note to lodge a strong complaint against Laos' intention to receive simultaneously two Vietnamese ambassadors to represent two Vietnamese regimes respectively in Vientiane. Laos offered to have the RVN ambassador remain in Vientiane, while opening a DRV diplomatic mission in Luang-Prabang. When talking about Laotian recognition of the Communist, Prince Souvanna Phouma claimed it was their duty as a neutral nation to have friendly relations with all the countries, and the South Vietnam's response was not of Laotian business. Diem was furious, and reacted by shutting its embassy in Vientiane.[521] The tension between Saigon and Vientiane troubled Washington as well, and President Kennedy requested a reconsideration of Diem's position. However, the US failed to persuade Diem to make Laos an exception, like the Soviet Union for the FRG.[522] The relations were not formally restored until 1965.

Alongside forging bilateral relations with individual states, the RVN devoted an extraordinary amount of energy and resources to actively participating in various international organizations and conferences. This was soundly reasoned by Diem's conviction that RVN's "chances of survival would be enhanced by systematic assertion of the regime's independent existence in the international arena, and by obtaining widespread recognition for its legal status as a sovereign entity under international law."[523] Above all, the RVN was keen to become a member of the United Nations. Its first attempt was made in 1957, with ten out of eleven states in the Security Council voting for the RVN's membership, which

---

520 Vietnam National Archives Center II, 1960.
521 Vietnam National Archives Center II, 1962.
522 Glennon, et al., 1990: 696–697.
523 Henderson and Fishel, 1966: 13.

was only blocked by Soviet's veto. And in various following votes on the admission of either or both of two Vietnams, the RVN had always garnered more votes. According to Bernard Fall, these were "impressive international testimonials to the regime's viability and to the validity of its claims to represent the Vietnamese people as a whole."[524] In addition to that, the RVN was a member of a large number of various kinds of international organizations, including UNESCO, WHO, UNICEF, IBRD, and IMF, to name but a few. Therefore, in turning down Hanoi's proposal, dated March 7, 1958, calling for normalizing relations between the North and the South, the government of RVN proudly declared that:

> "the democratic institutions established, and the progress achieved by our government in the political, economic and social fields have combined to win the support of foreign countries for the Republic of Vietnam. At the present time the nations which have extended recognition to our government, established diplomatic relations with us, or voted for our admission to the UN, number 56. As for the Communist authorities in the North, they have only obtained the recognition of about ten Communist governments. The prestige of our government has considerably increased during these past years: The Republic of Vietnam is at present member of 33 international organizations and Saigon has been chosen as the site of several international conferences."[525]

In general, as observed by Bernard Fall in 1967, the Republic of Vietnam had been far more successful than its northern counterpart in the game of international recognition, as it "has succeeded in gaining acceptance from countries of the Afro-Asian bloc to an extent the dour North Vietnamese rulers have thus far been unable to match."[526]

In the fierce competition between the RVN and the DRV, any success of one part would be considered as a loss of the other. The increased acceptance of the RVN in the international community only convinced the VWP leaders that they had to double their efforts before the South became too strong. In addition to that, Diem's campaign against communists seemed to be all too successful, which, in some southerners' judgment, would threaten the latter's survival in the South. Therefore, the VWP reoriented its policy to adopt a more militant line. Through 1959 and 1960, the VWP gradually rebuilt its strength in the South. On December 20, 1960, the National Liberation Front of South Vietnam came into being, which marked a threshold as the struggle in the South entering a new

524 Fall, 1967: 204–205.
525 Republic of Vietnam, 1961: 41–42.
526 Fall, 1967: 398.

stage of a revolutionary warfare. Consequently, the United States intervened in the defense of the Republic of Vietnam.

In hindsight, the United States was not that mighty. Meanwhile, the assassination of Ngo Dinh Diem in 1963 further worsened the situation of the RVN. The government broke into pieces, and the generals overthrowing Diem quickly began to fight against each other. It became chaotic, and no one could do anything. The Americans had to fight almost on their own.[527]

No matter how the United States justified its intervention in Vietnam, it was generally viewed as a violation of the principles of self-determination and non-intervention, and therefore, immoral. It undercut the American prestige established since President Wilson first appeared on the international stage, and also proved the incapacity and ineffectiveness of the RVN. In other words, by trying to save the RVN from imminent defeat, the United States undermined its long-term goal – the creation of an independent and noncommunist Vietnamese state. The more responsibilities the Americans assumed for shoring up the RVN government, the less credibility Saigon got.

By the end of 1960s, there was no doubt that the Vietnamese ultimately achieved their national independence and unification through the war. Nonetheless, diplomatic struggles "remained at the heart" and "proved no less important than the military and political ones."[528] After the presidential and parliamentary elections in 1967, Saigon embarked on another worldwide campaign to rebrand itself as a progressive alternative to Hanoi.[529] And the diplomatic competition continued in the shadow of once America's longest war.[530]

The DRV

To a certain extent, the Geneva Conference and its Agreements confirmed the existence and legitimacy of the Democratic Republic of Vietnam. In the aftermath of Geneva, no one would dare to call it "nothing more than an armed party."[531] On the contrary, Ho Chi Minh's government, with overwhelming

527 There were troops from other free world nations, but they were considered to be mercenaries paid by the United States, which was a practice not quite moral. Blackburn, 1994.
528 Asselin, 2013: 546.
529 Fear, 2018: 428.
530 Herring, 1996.
531 Szalontai, 2018: 33.

advantages over his counterpart in the South, now enjoyed great popularity and prestige both at home and abroad.[532]

As Vietnam was divided, the main objective of the Workers' Party was divided into two parts too: socialist transformation and the reunification of the nation. The party's cadres were divided as well: most northern leaders wanted to consolidate what were in control, while at the same time working toward national unification through political means. On the other hand, most southerners desired to liberate the South through a complete military victory. The northerners view dominated the party in the aftermath of Geneva.[533] In the period between 1954 and 1958, the VWP adopted wholeheartedly the policy of peaceful coexistence. There were three main tasks of their diplomacy: first and foremost, to strive for the implementation of the Geneva Agreements; second, to develop and maintain close relations with the fraternal countries; third, to broaden the relations with regional and nationalist countries.[534]

The first task failed. The Hanoi regime kept sending proposals for a consultative talk with Saigon, only to be rejected by the latter. Meanwhile the co-chairmen of the Geneva Conference were either unwilling or unable to enforce the Agreements. It became an illusion to achieve the unification of Vietnam in the ballot box. Ever since then, the Geneva Agreements were used as a propaganda weapon to gather the sympathy of the world opinion and to demoralize the position of Saigon and Washington.

The DRV also worked hard on the third task. Victories on battlefields along with the pragmatic behavior at the conference table created a great reputation for the DRV as the genuine nationalist, admired by a lot of Asian leaders, whether being Communist or not. Regardless of his vow for neutrality, Jawaharlal Nehru became the very first foreign head of state to visit Hanoi on October 17, 1954.[535] This was followed by another neutralist leader the Prime Minister of Burma U Nu, who visited Hanoi in November 1954 and signed a joint agreement with Ho Chi Minh to make the five principles of peaceful coexistence as the basis of bilateral relations. Albeit no full diplomatic relations, the Vietnamese viewed these

---

532 Thien, 1963: 132; Dommen, 2001: 260.

533 Brigham, 2000: 99–100.

534 Nguyen and Phung, 2010: 71.

535 It should be noticed that India carefully kept the balance between Hanoi and Saigon, as two weeks later, Nehru visited Saigon on October 30, 1954. Ngo Dinh Diem visited India from November 4 to 9, 1957. Later, Ho Chi Minh paid an official visit to India from February 5 to 13, 1958.

visits as a reflection of the solidarity between them and the peoples of India and Burma, which paved the way for friendly relations with other countries.[536]

The friendship with India and Burma ensured the DRV an entering ticket to the Afro-Asian Conference in 1955. The invitation itself was a demonstration of DRV's international prestige, for it was the only Communist regime besides the People's Republic of China – neither North Korea nor Mongolia was invited. Aware of the widespread desire for peace, the DRV delegation also relinquished its ideological language of class struggle and made peaceful coexistence the main theme of its address in Bandung. In addition, it praised the Geneva Conference as a great contribution to the peaceful coexistence of all nations with various backgrounds and systems.

> "The Geneva Conference was a great victory for the people of Viet-Nam, Cambodia and Laos. It was at the same time a great contribution to peace and to the struggle of the oppressed peoples. ...
>
> "The Geneva Agreements and the Final Declaration of the Conference have given official recognition to, and defined the practical steps to achieve national independence, national sovereignty, unity and territorial integrity of Viet-Nam, Cambodia and Laos. All participating countries to the Geneva Conference have undertaken to respect the legitimate rights of the peoples of Indochina to refrain from interfering in the internal affairs of the countries of Indochina and to express the confidence that from then on, Viet-Nam, Cambodia and Laos will be able fully to assume in full independence and sovereignty, their part in the peaceful community of nations."[537]

The delegates also expressed their government's desire to develop friendly relations with the Asian and African countries, with a special focus on the leading non-aligned countries – India, Burma, and Indonesia.

The DRV's attempt was only partly successful. Indonesia recognized the DRV and set up its Consulate in Hanoi on December 30, 1955. However, refraining from recognition and full diplomatic relations, India and Burma set General Consulates in Hanoi, respectively, and they had "all kinds of relations with Vietnam except legal and diplomatic."[538]

Another victory the DRV scored during this period came from Europe. As the tension reduced between the Soviet Union and Yugoslavia, Hanoi established ambassadorial relations with Belgrade on March 10, 1957.

From 1958 on, Hanoi began to reorient its strategy. This was a response to the unexpected development in the south – while the DRV consolidated in the

---

536 Pham, 1955: 40.
537 Centre for the Study of Asian-African Developing Countries, 1983: 121–122.
538 Misra, 1966: 71.

north, there was an independent and non-communist Vietnam in the making below the seventeenth parallel.

Starting from 1960, leaders in the Democratic Republic of Vietnam decided to fight for the reunification through revolutionary warfare. The VWP's diplomatic activities were pushed up to serve the revolution in the South, through mobilizing support and assistance from the Soviet Union and China, denouncing the US war scheme and garnering sympathy and support from people all over the world. This diplomacy was fruitful. On the one hand, it made its appeal heard by the world, and gathered widespread international support and voluminous material assistance from the Soviet Union and China in spite of the increasingly intensified conflict between these two communist giants. On the other hand, it undermined the position of the US and the RVN. In the context of decolonization, the image of "a microbe facing a leviathan,"[539] in other words, a poor farming nation fighting against the richest and the strongest nation, attracted the attention of the whole world, and presented the Vietnamese as an admiration of the undeveloped world and an inspiration for national independence.

As the war prolonged, more and more people became sympathetic to the DRV. In January 1969, Sweden became the first Western nation to grant full diplomatic recognition to the DRV and establish diplomatic relations with it under the risk of potential American economic sanctions. Leaders in Stockholm objected to the American intervention for moral, legal, and geostrategic reasons; and by recognizing the DRV, they fashioned an independent policy on the war, and made their voices heard by the world.[540] Others gradually and cautiously followed suit in the early 1970s, and not surprisingly, the neutrals moved faster than the rest European countries.

The competition for diplomatic recognition was eventually disentangled by the reunification of Vietnam on April 30, 1975. From July 2, 1976 onward, there is one and only Vietnam, namely the Socialist Republic of Vietnam. It became a member of the United Nations in 1977, and now has diplomatic relations with 180 countries.[541]

Summary

Recalling history, it is interesting to notice that the superpowers were not unhesitant in recognizing Vietnam. In fact, during its first four-and-half-year existence,

---

539 Karnow, 1984: 435.
540 Logevall, 1993: 435–437.
541 Press and Information Department, 2013.

the Democratic Republic of Vietnam failed to gain even a single recognition. The situation was desperate – on the one hand, the Soviet was dubious about Ho Chi Minh's loyalty to communism; on the other hand, the West questioned whether Ho was a genuine nationalist or not. The very first "yes" vote came the People's Republic of China. Still, the superpowers held the final saying. The Soviet Union formally recognized the DRV in the end of January 1950, followed by the United States extending recognition of the State of Vietnam in early February. Once the stage was set, the United States wasted no time in recognizing the Republic of Vietnam on the very day it was founded. No one wanted to bear the responsibility of dividing Vietnam, but no one could be excused from it.

Standing at the front line of the East-West conflict, Vietnam attracted attention everywhere. When thinking about establishing diplomatic relations with either the RVN or the DRV, most states held the line and stuck to their bloc solidarity. All the countries of the Soviet bloc stood solemnly with the DRV; meanwhile none of the Western countries – including all the European neutral states – recognized the DRV before 1969.

Generally speaking, the newly independent states in Asia and Africa preferred to treat the RVN and the DRV equally, following the model set by India and Burma. This policy is understandable, for the newcomers weighted their status as an independent state in the international system and did not want to be involved in the conflict of the developed countries. It was only the US intervention that tipped the balance in the DRV's favor.

To be frankly, the Second Republic (1967–1975) was in chaos from beginning to end. There was no surprise that the RVN did not make any achievement during this period. However, the RVN was able to stay ahead in the diplomatic arena on the sheet till 1973, as shown in Figure 5-12, thanks to the strong support from the United States.

Nearly twenty years after the stillborn of national elections promised in Geneva, Vietnam eventually achieved its independence and unification.

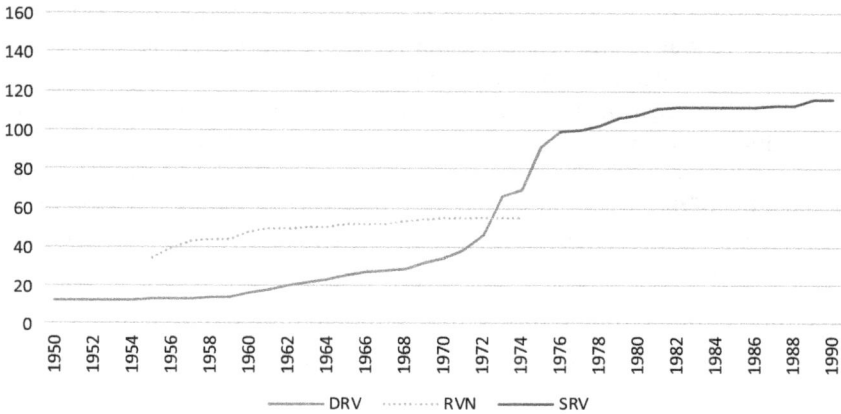

Figure 5-12. Vietnam: Diplomatic Recognition, 1950–1990

5.5. A Wider Picture

The Cold War was predominantly characterized by the rivalry between the United States and the Soviet Union in all aspects. The two superpowers defined their respective sphere of influence, and hence divided the globe into different blocs. The confrontational nature of the Cold War bipolarity made sure that every political entity of divided nations would be recognized by a certain number of states while none of them could manage to achieve universal recognition.

In a nutshell, the Warsaw Pact countries were more unified than the NATO members. Recognition of the Communist parts of divided nations normally came immediately after their foundation, with the only exception of the DRV – the Cold War only arrived at its doorstep five years after its proclamation; but once connected, recognition followed.

Meanwhile, the American friends and allies had a huge advantage in numbers. Therefore, the anti-Communist regimes were more likely to take the lead in the diplomatic competition.

As for those outside the two blocs, things were not that straightforward. For instance, though deeply committed to neutrality, Switzerland recognized the PRC on January 17, 1950, but maintained official relations only with the non-Communist parts of Germany, Korea, and Vietnam for a decade or longer. The European neutrals were Western neutrals, and their one-sided neutrality would no doubt undermine the credibility of neutrality.[542] In contrast, the non-aligned nations in Asia and Africa showed a more balanced attitude, at least towards the more evenly divided Korea and Vietnam.

Due to the high intensity of confrontation between the two blocs, cross-recognition was almost impossible to reach during the 1950s and 1960s. The major exceptions were the British recognition of the PRC in 1950, the Soviet recognition of the FRG in 1955, and then the French recognition of the PRC in 1964. More or less, these actions weakened the solidarity within their blocs, and undermined the leadership of the superpowers.

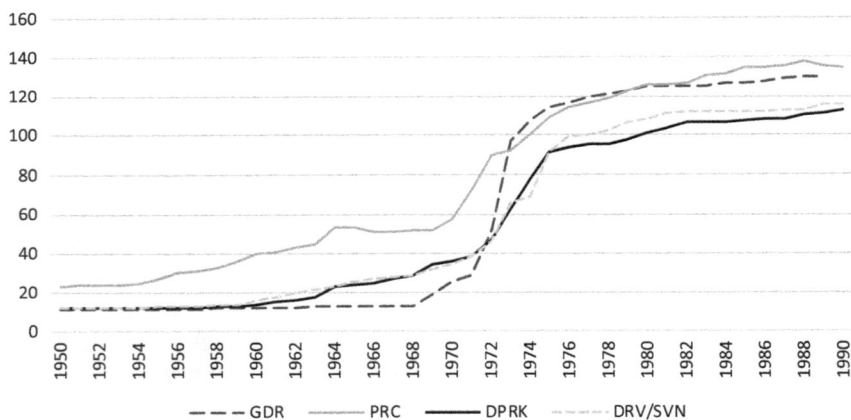

Figure 5-13. Diplomatic Recognition of Communist Regimes

---

542 Schaufelbuehl, et al., 2015: 1029.

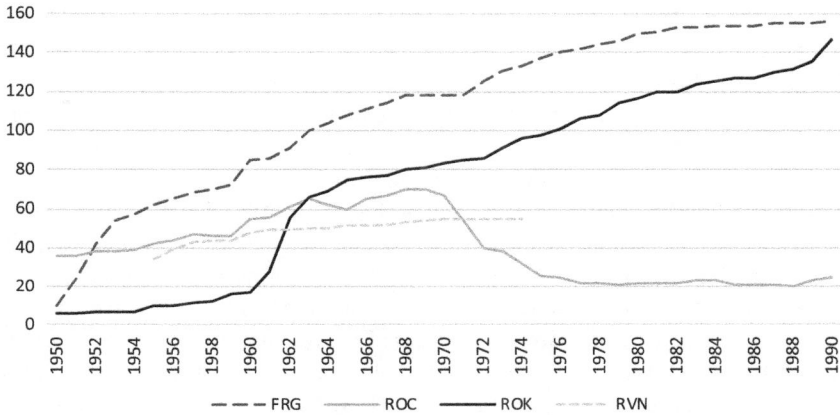

Figure 5-14. Diplomatic Recognition of Non-Communist Regimes

Since 1969, the tension between the two blocs became relaxed. The super-powers, especially the United States, no longer opposed the recognition of the other parts of divided nations. Alongside the Détente, the FRG and the GDR recognized each other as a separate state in 1972, while the two Koreas raised no more objections to diplomatic recognition by third parties. Therefore, during the 1970s, all the four Communist regimes made dramatic progress in diplomatic recognition, as presented in Figure 5-13. Nonetheless, the Détente did not nec-essarily lead to dual recognition, as the ROC experienced a rapid decline, while the RVN was totally taken over, as illustrated in Figure 5-14.

It is worthy pointing out that for most countries, recognition is a matter that will only be encountered once in a lifetime. The renewed tension between the two superpowers since 1979 did not lead to any de-recognition of these states. Furthermore, as time passed, the regime durability became evident, which would make any policy shift back to non-recognition ridiculous.

So far, it is confirmed that the international factors have a great influence on the diplomatic recognition of political entities suffering national division.

Aside from that, national-level factors were also significant. States with a big-ger area and a larger population usually have a greater capacity to enter into foreign relations, and therefore are more likely to score higher on the diplomatic sheet. When only one is allowed to be chosen from two competing regimes, the larger one generally has a better chance to be picked up.

Throughout this period, the FRG was the most democratic. And apart from the very first few years of its establishment, the FRG was also the most widely recognized. This phenomenon fits well with the quantitative analysis, in which the level of democracy is statistically significant. However, this is only a correlation without clear causal link. For other regimes, none of their diplomatic breakthroughs came after domestic democratization.

It is noteworthy that in the aftermath of the Second World War, nationalism – especially in its expansionist form – was considered to be the cause of the wars. And the Allies were not hesitant in dividing some nations, in order to keep their respective spheres of influence.[543] Nonetheless, none of such divided nations accepted willingly such a division. Nationalism remains to be the basic organizing principle. Most of these regimes deliver reunification on top of policy goals, and are devoted to achieving such goals by its own term. It is still a system of nation-states.

---

543 Barkin and Cronin, 1994: 122–125.

Chapter 6 General Conclusion

Recognition has been a long-debated topic in public international law since the early nineteenth century, and it became more popular in the discipline of international relations thanks, in no small part, to the efforts of the constructivists. By summarizing the various discussions about recognition, I consider recognition to be the most fundamental interaction in diplomatic practice. It begins with the self-identification of political entities. To be recognized by others means not only that they are accepted as an equal member of the international system, but also that their claims about who they are, what their role in the world is, and where they govern are acknowledged – if not supported, at least not challenged. These are such fundamental questions; they are simply key to understanding any individual entity.

In daily practices, recognition has often been mixed up with the establishment of diplomatic relations and/or the exchange of ambassadors, therefore it is often overlooked. However, for those whose statehood is in question, recognition is a matter of life and death. It became paramount as the iron curtain descended, the world was divided, and those nations living on the front line suffered the most. They struggled, for physical survival and ontological security as well.

China, as a long-standing civilization, had experienced Western Imperialism since the Opium War. China's arduous resistance against the Japanese invasion earned its status as a big power in the world order after the Second World War. However, China was economically weak and politically fragmented in 1945, and the Civil War soon re-ignited. Mao Zedong proclaimed the founding of the People's Republic of China in October 1949, while Jiang Jieshi's Republic of China retreated to Taiwan. Because of the American intervention, they were unable to cross the Taiwan Strait and overcome their opponent on the battlefield. Ever since the founding of the KMT and the CCP in the early twentieth century, the two parties have devoted much of their efforts to portraying themselves as the savor of the Chinese nation, and neither of them could afford the undermining of national integrity. Both the PRC and the ROC claim to be the sole legitimate government of China, which results in an on-going dispute.

Germany's destiny was in the hands of the Allies. Germany was too important from a geostrategic point of view. While a united and independent Germany might threaten everyone on the continent, a united Germany in alliance with others was also an unimaginable scenario. Therefore, the division of Germany became inevitable under these circumstances. The Federal Republic of Germany was founded in May 1949, followed by the proclamation of the German Democratic Republic in October that year. The FRG claimed to be the sole legitimate representative of the entire German people, whereas the GDR made the same assertion but changed its course in 1955, and from then on purported to be the better Germany and sought to be recognized as another German state; their competition to win international recognition was described by Gray as "Germany's Cold War."[544]

Korea was to become a free and independent country in due course after the defeat of Japan. However, when the Japanese surrendered in 1945, the United States and the Soviet Union hastily divided the peninsula along the thirty-eighth parallel. As the tension of the Cold War increased, negotiation on unification failed in 1948, resulting in the establishment of two separate governments – the Democratic People's Republic of Korea in the north, and the Republic of Korea in the south. Kim Il Sung wanted to unite the peninsula by force, thus ignited the Korean War in June 1950. The war was soon internationalized. After a protracted ebb and flow, it reached a stalemate and unofficially ended in an armistice on July 27, 1953. Since the 1970s, the two Koreas raised no more opposition against the recognition of each other by foreign nations. Nonetheless, both North and South Korea claimed to represent the entire peninsula and never gave up the pursuit of reunification.

Vietnam was a French colony before the Second World War, and the Allies agreed to return it to France. However, after the defeat of Japan, the Viet Minh published the Proclamation of Independence and established the Democratic Republic of Vietnam in September 1945. The Viet Minh defeated the French in 1954, then the Geneva Agreements were signed, and, according to their stipulations, Vietnam was divided at the seventeenth parallel. The DRV was secured, but the general elections promised by the Geneva Agreements were never implemented. Instead, the Republic of Vietnam was established in the south in 1955. However, Ngo Dinh Diem's project of building a free and independent Vietnam was terminated with his assassination in 1963. The situation deteriorated rapidly and the war escalated, and the large-scale American involvement further undercut any claims that the RVN was an independent sovereign state. After the Americans withdrew, DRV forces eventually seized control of the whole of Vietnam. It took two decades to achieve the promised unification, and the price had been extremely high.

---

544 Gray, 2003.

Based on the quantitative analysis and comparative study I have undertaken with regard to these four cases, some general conclusions can be drawn: first and foremost, the international system has a great influence on the diplomatic recognition of divided nations. The Cold War logic generally predetermined the recognition policies of the majority of the established countries. During the heydays of the Cold War, the Communist regimes were barely recognized by their bloc members, while the non-Communist regimes generally enjoyed more widespread diplomatic recognition. Since the late 1960s, the two superpowers relaxed the tensions between them, and also loosened control among their respective friends and allies, which brought more fluidity to the recognition dynamics of divided nations.

Generally speaking, the trend during the period from 1950 to 1990 was in favor of the maintenance of established borders.[545] And in the case of divided nations, once the two parts accepted the dividing line as a border (even in a temporary manner), other states would recognize them as two states, whether in one nation or not.

However, dual recognition is impossible so long as any part of the divided nation in question upholds the principle of national integrity and opposes the recognition of its rival. States normally prefer to grant recognition to the stronger half when choosing sides. Even those Western countries singing the praises of democratic values showed no evidence of making the standard of democracy the cornerstone of their recognition decisions.

As mentioned before, these dynamics are neither exclusive nor exhaustive. Economic factors are potential candidates, too. Economic incentives have proven effective even in the highly militarized and ideologically polarized period of the Cold War.[546] The purchase of recognition continues, for instance, Beijing and Taipei blamed each other for engaging in "checkbook diplomacy" until Ma Yingjiu proposed a policy of diplomatic truce in 2008, but the diplomatic warfare resumed after Ma's exit in 2016. Although foreign aid is a useful tool for buying recognition, it is difficult to obtain data concerning the aid projects promised and completed. This aspect still needs to be explored further.

It is important to point out that before the Second World War, recognition was generally perceived as a unilateral act taken by an existing state, hence a privilege reserved for the well-established Western countries. However, during

---

545 Barkin and Cronin, 1994: 123.
546 Newnham, 2000.

the period from 1950 to 1990, the rivaling political entities engaged in a grand struggle to garner recognition from every corner of the globe.

Their competition for recognition got entangled with the process of decolonization. After the Second World War, colonialism had become discredited, and was eventually outlawed by the United Nations General Assembly Resolution 1514.[547] As a result, the post-war era witnessed a vast expansion of the international society. And for these newly independent states, in Sub-Sahara Africa in particular, recognition became "a wholesale transaction," described by Gerard Kreijen as "a mere cordial cognitive act, which – characteristically – was at times even granted in anticipation."[548] In other words, these newcomers were entitled to recognition as the logic consequence of their right to self-determination. Recognition indeed befell automatically under the decolonizing circumstances. The once exclusive club of sovereign states promptly opened up to all the nations.

Traditionally, recognition is granted by the established to the newly emerging. Here, we find the situation reversed, as these rivaling regimes of divided nations sought to win recognition from the newcomers. Though many of them were unprepared at the very beginning, these newcomers would have to take a position in these recognition contests eventually. And their recognition decisions would no doubt reflect their understandings about who they are and their perceptions of the world. As these decolonized states poured onto the international stage, recognition would no longer be dictated by only one or two Western powers.

Individually speaking, the newly independent African and Asian states were weak and small, but together they made up a majority in the United Nations, which could create a sort of international public opinion that no great power could keep ignoring. A good example of this was the Chinese representation issue. As mentioned before, the United States had been successful in rallying a clear majority to prevent the entry of the PRC in the 1950s. Then, as more and more African and Asian states joined the United Nations, it changed its tactic of "important matter" in the 1960s. In the end, the United States had to give up its stance in 1971. Some might argue that the expulsion of the ROC is a result of the Sino-American rapprochement. As a matter of fact, the Resolution 2758 was adopted by the UN General Assembly on October 25, 1971, ahead of Nixon's trip to China. And the Chinese Communists were rather caught by surprise.[549]

---

547 United Nations General Assembly, 1960.
548 Kreijen, 2004: 369.
549 Liu, 2014: 49.

Dealing with the divided nations, the newly independent states were moderately more sympathetic to their national sufferings and less affected by Cold War ideology. Appreciating their independence and sovereignty, they sought to claim their agency in international affairs and yet stand independent of bloc politics.[550] In fact, many of them found common attachment in anti-imperialism. According to James Mayall, nationalism in Africa and Asia was by and large a reaction to imperial conquest.[551] As already demonstrated in Bandung in 1955, the African and Asian nations condemned all kinds of colonialism – not only the formal colonialism of the Western European empires, but also the Soviet informal empire in East Europe and the neocolonialism of the United States.[552] Seen from a Third World perspective, the Cold War was nothing but a continuation of colonialism under a slightly new cover. It is in this way that Mao Zedong and Ho Chi Minh became attractive role models for many Third World leaders, setting the example of taking actions for and by themselves, in spite of American military dominance or Soviet political doctrine.[553]

After the sudden collapse of the Soviet bloc, the Cold War ended in Western triumphalism. The GDR was absorbed by the FRG in 1990. The ROK today enjoys economic prosperity and became a member of the G20. There has been quite a lot of discussion about applying the German reunification model to Korea ever since the early 1990s.[554] The DPRK only survives as a pariah state, but no one would hesitate to categorize it as a state.

Even though it experienced successful democratic reform and economic development, the ROC became further marginalized on the international stage. The ROC, or Taiwan, nowadays frequently appears on the list of de facto states, and, as such, has been in a problematic status ever since.[555]

How about these de facto states forming an alliance and exchange recognition among themselves? Would it create a scenario similar to that of inside bloc recognition among the Communist regimes during the early years of the Cold War? My answer is a clear no. Because most of them are small and weak, with no superpower to bind them together. Putin's Russia is not so capable as the Soviet Union. Russia can recognize the statelets, for instance, Abkhazia, South Ossetia, Transnistria, Donetsk and Luhansk; however, its influence is also limited to the

---

550 Ewing, 2019: 2.
551 Mayall, 1990: 2.
552 Berger, 2004: 12.
553 Westad, 2005: 158–160.
554 Rhee, 1993; Jonsson, 2017; Lee and Moon, 2020.
555 Kolstø, 2006; Florea, 2014.

surrounding area, and it can hardly trigger wide diplomatic recognition beyond the former Soviet region. The PRC might be a challenger to the United States, but it is by no means challenging the international system or creating a sub-system of its own. On the contrary, the PRC is committed to maintaining the stability of the international system and safeguarding the integrity of the territorial sovereignty. As shown in the recent events, Beijing always attempts to remain neutral and refrains from recognizing any breakaway state. On the other side, Taipei comes with a fatal flaw attached where recognizing it as a state is concerned, as anyone that seeks universal recognition would need to be careful not to infuriate Beijing.

In general, the international system is status quo-biased, preferring the preservation of the established boundaries between states. It has been argued by Michael Hechter that "If there is one constant in history apart from the universality of death and taxes, it is the reluctance of states to part with territory."[556] The norm of territorial integrity is widespread, which functions as a protective shield for established states. The international system is a system of states and for states.

Focusing on the issue of border fixity, Boaz Arzili argues that the concept of survival is no longer relevant, for states simply survive and do not die anymore.[557] However, for that of divided nations, the threat is real. They keep struggling for their survival, both psychical and psychological.

---

556 Hechter, 1992: 277.
557 Atzili, 2012: 218.

List of Figures

List of Tables

Bibliography

Adenauer K (1965) *Erinnerungen [1]: 1945–1953.* Stuttgart: Deutsche Verlags-Anstalt.

Ahonen P (2003) *After the Expulsion: West Germany and Eastern Europe, 1945–1990.* Oxford; New York: Oxford University Press.

Alesina A and Spolaore E (2005) *The Size of Nations.* MIT Press.

Anderson BROG (2006) *Imagined Communities: Reflections on the Origin and Spread of Nationalism.* London: Verso.

Anderson G (2015) Unilateral Non-Colonial Secession and the Criteria for Statehood in International Law. *Brooklyn Journal of International Law* 41(1): 1–98.

Anordnung Über Das Betreten Der Hauptstadt Der Deutschen Demokratischen Republik Berlin (Das Demokratische Berlin) Durch Bürger Der Deutschen Bundesrepublik. (1960) *Neues Deutschland*, August 31, 1960, 1.

Archives of the Ministry of Foreign Affairs (2006a) 1954 Nian Ri Nei Wa Hui Yi [1954 Geneva Conference]. *Zhonghua Renmin Gongheguo Wai Jiao Dang an Xuan Bian.* Beijing: Shi jie zhi shi chu ban she.

Archives of the Ministry of Foreign Affairs (2006b) *Jie Mi Wai Jiao Wen Xian: Zhong Hua Ren Min Gong He Guo Jian Jiao Dang An: 1949–1955 [Declassification of Diplomatic Archives: Files on Establishing Diplomatic Relations of People's Republic of China: 1949–1955].* Beijing: China Pictorial Publishing House.

Archives of the Ministry of Foreign Affairs (2007) Zhong Guo Dai Biao Tuan Chu Xi 1955 Nian Ya Fei Hui Yi [Chinese Delegation Attending the Afro-Asian Conference of 1955]. *Zhonghua Renmin Gongheguo Wai Jiao Dang an Xuan Bian.* Beijing: Shi jie zhi shi chu ban she.

Armstrong CK (2001) America's Korea, Korea's Vietnam. *Critical Asian Studies* 33(4): 527–540.

Armstrong CK (2013) *Tyranny of the Weak: North Korea and the World, 1950–1992.* Ithaca; London: Cornell University Press.

Asselin P (2013) *Hanoi's Road to the Vietnam War, 1954–1965.* Berkeley: University of California Press.

Atzili B (2012) *Good Fences, Bad Neighbors: Border Fixity and International Conflict.* Chicago; London: University of Chicago Press.

Außenministerkonferenz Der Staaten Des Warschauer Vertrages Beendet: Atmosphäre Kameradschaftlicher Zusammenarbeit Und Völligen Einvernehmens. (1967) *Neues Deutschland*, February 11, 1967, 1.

Badarin E (2020) States Recognition in Foreign Policy: The Case of Sweden's Recognition of Palestine. *Foreign Policy Analysis* 16(1): 78–97.

Bailes AJK (2015) Legal Precision or Fuzzy Feelings? A Diplomatic Comment on Recognition Studies. In: Daase C, Fehl C, Geis A, et al. (eds) *Recognition in International Relations. Rethinking a Political Concept in a Global Context*. Basingstoke, Hampshire: Palgrave Macmillan, pp. 251–264.

Banerjee S (1997) The Cultural Logic of National Identity Formation: Contending Discourses in Late Colonial India. In: Hudson VM (ed) *Culture and Foreign Policy*. Boulder; London: Lynne Rienner Publishers, pp. 27–44.

Bange O (2016) Onto the Slippery Slope: East Germany and East-West Détente under Ulbricht and Honecker, 1965–1975. *Journal of Cold War Studies* 18(3): 60–94.

Barkin JS and Cronin B (1994) The State and the Nation: Changing Norms and the Rules of Sovereignty in International Relations. *International Organization* 48(1): 107–130.

Beitrag Zur Festigung Des Friedens in Europa. (1957) *Neues Deutschland*, October 16, 1957, 1.

Berger MT (2004) After the Third World? History, Destiny and the Fate of Third Worldism. *Third World Quarterly* 25(1): 9–39.

Bernhard M (2001) Democratization in Germany: A Reappraisal. *Comparative Politics*. 379–400.

Beschloss MR (1991) *The Crisis Years: Kennedy and Khrushchev 1960–1963*. New York: Burlingame Books.

Blackburn RM (1994) *Mercenaries and Lyndon Johnson's "More Flags": The Hiring of Korean, Filipino and Thai Soldiers in the Vietnam War*. Jefferson, N.C.: McFarland.

Booz RM (1995) *"Hallsteinzeit": Deutsche Außenpolitik; 1955–1972*. Bonn: Bouvier.

Brautigam D (2009) *The Dragon's Gift: The Real Story of China in Africa*. Oxford; New York: Oxford University Press.

Brazinsky GA (2017) *Winning the Third World: Sino-American Rivalry During the Cold War*. Chapel Hill: The University of North Carolina Press.

Bridges B (2008) The Seoul Olympics: Economic Miracle Meets the World. *The International Journal of the History of Sport* 25(14): 1939–1952.

Brierly JL (1963) *The Law of Nations: An Introduction to the International Law of Peace*. Oxford: Oxford University Press.

Briggs HW (1950) Community Interest in the Emergence of New States: The Problem of Recognition. *Proceedings of the American Society of International Law at Its Annual Meeting* 44: 169–181.

Brigham RK (2000) Vietnam at the Center: Patterns of Diplomacy and Resistance. In: Gardner LC and Gittinger T (eds) *International Perspectives on Vietnam*. College Station: Texas A & M University Press.

Brown IJC (1920) *The Meaning of Democracy*. London: Richard Cobden-Sanderson.

Brownlie I (1983) Recognition in Theory and Practice. In: St. Macdonald RJ and Johnston DM (eds) *The Structure and Process of International Law. Essays in Legal Philosophy, Doctrine and Theory*. The Hague; Lancaster: Nijhoff, pp. 627–742.

Bull H (2012) *The Anarchical Society: A Study of Order in World Politics*. Macmillan International Higher Education.

Bull H and Watson A (1984) *The Expansion of International Society*. Oxford: Clarendon Press.

Burr W (1994) Avoiding the Slippery Slope: The Eisenhower Administration and the Berlin Crisis, November 1958-January 1959. *Diplomatic History* 18(2): 177–205.

Buzan B (2014) The "Standard of Civilisation" as an English School Concept. *Millennium: Journal of International Studies* 42(3): 576–594.

Campbell J (2019) Strapped for Cash, Nigeria Plans to Close Some Embassies. In: Council on Foreign Relations. Available at: https://www.cfr.org/blog/nige ria-security-tracker-weekly-update-may-18-24 (accessed July 28, 2020).

Carr EH (1947) *Conditions of Peace*. New York: Macmillan.

Caspersen N (2012) *Unrecognized States: The Struggle for Sovereignty in the Modern International System*. Cambridge: Polity Press.

Caspersen N (2018) Recognition, Status Quo or Reintegration: Engagement with De Facto States. *Ethnopolitics* 17(4): 373–389.

Centre for the Study of Asian-African Developing Countries (1983) *Collected Documents of the Asian-African Conference: April 18–24, 1955*. Jakarta: Agency for Research and Development, The Department of Foreign Affairs.

Chapman JM (2006) Staging Democracy: South Vietnam's 1955 Referendum to Depose Bao Dai. *Diplomatic History* 30(4): 671–703.

Chen J (1997) *China's Road to the Korean War: The Making of the Sino-American Confrontation*. New York; Chichester: Columbia University Press.

Chen J and Shen Z (2008) The Geneva Conference of 1954: New Evidence from the Archives of the Ministry of Foreign Affairs of the People's Republic of China. *Cold War International History Project Bulletin* 16: 7–84.

Chen KC (1969) *Vietnam and China, 1938–1954*. Princeton, N.J.: Princeton University Press.

Chen T-C (1951) *The International Law of Recognition: With Special Reference to Practice in Great Britain and the United States*. New York: Praeger.

Cho SS (1967) The Politics of North Korea's Unification Policies 1950–1965. *World Politics* 19(2): 218–241.

Choi SJ (1984) *Diplomatic Recognition Problems of a Divided Nation: The Case of Korea*. Doctoral Dissertation, University of Notre Dame.

Chou L (2001) The Diplomatic War between Beijing and Taipei in Chile. *Maryland Series in Contemporary Asian Studies* 164(3): 1–61.

Chung C (1986) North Korea and the International Community: The Search for Legitimacy in the United Nations and Elsewhere. In: Scalapino RA and Lee H (eds) *North Korea in a Regional and Global Context*. Berkeley, C.A.: University of California Press, pp. 344–370.

Clare KG, Foster GJ, Hannus RC, et al. (1969) *Area Handbook for the Republic of Korea*. Washington, D.C.: United States Government Printing Office.

Clark I (2005) *Legitimacy in International Society*. Oxford: Oxford University Press.

Clark I (2009) Democracy in International Society: Promotion or Exclusion? *Millennium: Journal of International Studies* 37(3): 563–581.

Clark II KA (2018) Imagined Territory: The Republic of China's 1955 Veto of Mongolian Membership in the United Nations. *The Journal of American-East Asian Relations* 25(3): 263–295.

Claude IL (1966) Collective Legitimization as a Political Function of the United Nations. *International Organization* 20(3): 367–379.

Clough RN (1978) *Island China*. Cambridge, Massachusetts: Harvard University Press.

Clough RN (1987) *Embattled Korea: The Rivalry for International Support*. Boulder: Westview Press.

Coggins B (2014) *Power Politics and State Formation in the Twentieth Century: The Dynamics of Recognition*. Cambridge: Cambridge University Press.

Cohen SB (2015) *Geopolitics: The Geography of International Relations*. Lanham: Rowman & Littlefield.

Colbert ES (1977) *Southeast Asia in International Politics, 1941–1956*. Ithaca; London: Cornell University Press.

Coleman A (2014) The Islamic State and International Law: An Ideological Rollercoster? *Journal of The Philosophy of International Law* 5(2): 75–80.

Correlates of War (2013) Formal Alliance, V4.1. Available at: http://correlatesof war.org (August 15, 2019).

Correlates of War (2017a) National Material Capabilities, V5.0. Available at: http://correlatesofwar.org (August 15, 2019).

Correlates of War (2017b) State System Membership List, V2016. Available at: http://correlatesofwar.org (August 15, 2019).

Crawford J (2006) *The Creation of States in International Law*. Oxford: Clarendon Press.

Cummins I (1980) *Marx, Engels and National Movements*. London: Croom Helm.

Das Gupta AR (2014) The Non-Aligned and the German Question. In: Miskovic N, Fischer-Tine H and Boskovska N (eds) *Non-Aligned Movement and the Cold War: Delhi – Bandung – Belgrade*. New York, NY: Routledge, pp. 143–160.

Das Gupta AR (2019) The Fateful Indian Recognition of West Germany, 1949. *Cold War History* 19(1): 101–117.

Deighton A (1990) *The Impossible Peace: Britain, the Division of Germany and the Origins of Cold War*. Oxford: Clarendon Press.

Deng X (1993) *Selected Works of Deng Xiaoping, Vol. 3 (1982–1992)*. Beijing: People's Publishing House.

Deuerlein E (1961) *Dokumente Zur Deutschlandpolitik: III. Reihe/Band 1: 5. Mai Bis 31. Dezember 1955*. Frankfurt am Main: Metzner.

DiGangi RL, Lees L, Miller A, et al. (1992) *Foreign Relations of the United States, 1955-1957, Central and Southeastern Europe, Volume XXVI*. Washington, D.C.: United States Government Printing Office.

Dittmer L and Kim SS (2018) In Search of a Theory of National Identity. In: Dittmer L and Kim SS (eds) *China's Quest for National Identity*. Ithaca, NY: Cornell University Press, pp. 1–31.

Do J (2020) North Korean "Independence" in Unification Policy and Sino-North Korean Relations, 1955–1966. *Asian Perspective* 44(3): 513–534.

Dommen AJ (2001) *The Indochinese Experience of the French and the Americans: Nationalism and Communism in Cambodia, Laos, and Vietnam*. Bloomington, IN: Indiana University Press.

Dozer DM (1966) Recognition in Contemporary Inter-American Relations. *Journal of Inter-American Studies* 8(2): 318–335.

Dugard J (1987) *Recognition and the United Nations*. Cambridge: Grotius.

Dunn J (1979) *Western Political Theory in the Face of the Future*. Cambridge: Cambridge University Press.

Eberstadt N (2010) *Policy and Economic Performance in Divided Korea During the Cold War Era: 1945-91.* Washington, D.C.: AEI Press.

Economic Aid for S.E. Asia: Discussions at Colombo. (1950) *The Times*, January 13, 1950, 4.

Eisenberg CW (1996) *Drawing the Line: The American Decision to Divide Germany, 1944-1949.* Cambridge: Cambridge University Press.

Engerman DC (2010) Ideology and the Origins of the Cold War, 1917-1962. In: Leffler MP and Westad OA (eds) *The Cambridge History of the Cold War.* Cambridge; New York: Cambridge University Press, pp. 20-43.

Europäische Sicherheit Erfordert Verzicht Auf Revanchepolitik. (1967) *Neues Deutschland*, February 3, 1967, 1.

Europe's Populists Are Waltzing into the Mainstream. (2018) *The Economist*, Feburuary 3, 2018.

European Community: Declaration on Yugoslavia and on the Guidelines on the Recognition of New States. (1992) *International Legal Materials* 31(6): 1485-1487.

Ewing C (2019) The Colombo Powers: Crafting Diplomacy in the Third World and Launching Afro-Asia at Bandung. *Cold War History* 19(1): 1-19.

Fabry M (2010) *Recognizing States: International Society and the Establishment of New States since 1776.* Oxford: Oxford University Press.

Fabry M (2020) The Evolution of State Recognition. In: Visoka G, Doyle J and Newman E (eds) *Routledge Handbook of State Recognition.* London: Routledge, pp. 37-47.

Fall BB (1967) *The Two Viet-Nams: A Political and Military Analysis.* New York: Praeger.

Fear S (2018) Saigon Goes Global: South Vietnam's Quest for International Legitimacy in the Age of Détente. *Diplomatic History* 42(3): 428-455.

Feldkamp MF (2008) *Der Parlamentarische Rat 1948-1949: Die Entstehung Des Grundgesetzes.* Göttingen: Vandenhoeck & Ruprecht.

Fidler DP (2000) A Kinder, Gentler System of Capitulations?: International Law, Structural Adjustment Policies, and the Standard of Liberal, Globalized Civilization. *Texas International Law Journal* 35: 387-413.

Fink C (2019) *West Germany and Israel: Foreign Relations, Domestic Politics, and the Cold War, 1965-1974.* Cambridge: Cambridge University Press.

Finkelstein DM (1993) *Washington's Taiwan Dilemma: From Abandonment to Salvation.* Fairfax, VA: George Mason University Press.

Florea A (2014) De Facto States in International Politics (1945-2011): A New Data Set. *International Interactions* 40(5): 788-811.

Foreign Office (1965) *Documents Relating to British Involvement in the Indo-China Conflict: 1945–1965*. London: Her Majesty's Stationery Office.

Foucault M (2009) *Security, Territory, and Population: Lectures at the Collège De France, 1977–1978*. New York, NY: Palgrave Macmillan.

Freeman CW (2020) China's National Experiences and the Evolution of PRC Grand Strategy. In: Shambaugh DL (ed) *China and the World*. Oxford: Oxford University Press, pp. 37–60.

Friedman J (2015) *Shadow Cold War: The Sino-Soviet Competition for the Third World*. Chapel Hill: The University of North Carolina Press.

Gao L (1993) *Zhong Hua Min Guo Wai Jiao Guan Xi Zhi Yan Bian, 1950–1972 [the Evolution of the Republic of China's Foreign Relations, 1950–1972]*. Taipei: Wu-nan Book.

Geldenhuys D (2009) *Contested States in World Politics*. New York: Palgrave Macmillan.

Gellner E (2007) *Nations and Nationalism*. Oxford: Blackwell.

Gibler DM (2009) *International Military Alliances, 1648–2008*. Washington, D.C.: CQ Press.

Gilbert MJ (2002) Introduction. In: Gilbert MJ (ed) *Why the North Won the Vietnam War. New Interpretations*. New York: Palgrave, pp. 1–45.

Gills BK (1996) *Korea Versus Korea: A Case of Contested Legitimacy*. Florence: Routledge.

Girault R (1986) The French Decision-Makers and Their Perception of French Power in 1948. In: Becker J and Knipping F (eds) *Power in Europe. Great Britain, France, Italy and Germany in a Postwar World, 1945–1950*. Berlin; New York: De Gruyter, pp. 47–65.

Glanville L (2013) The Myth of "Traditional" Sovereignty. *International Studies Quarterly* 57(1): 79–90.

Glennon JP (1976) *Foreign Relations of the United States, 1950, Korea, Volume Vii*. Washington, D.C.: United States Government Printing Office.

Glennon JP, Baehler DM and Sampson CS (1990) *Foreign Relations of the United States, 1961–1963, Volume II, Vietnam, 1962*. Washington, D.C.: United States Government Printing Office.

Gong GW (1984) *The Standard of "Civilization" in International Society*. Oxford: Clarendon Press.

Goodrich LM (1956) *Korea: A Study of U.S. Policy in the United Nations*. New York: Council on Foreign Relations.

Goodwin RR, Kane NS and Schwar HD (1979) *Foreign Relations of the United States, 1951, the United Nations; the Western Hemisphere, Volume II.* Washington, D.C.: United States Government Printing Office.

Goodwin RR, Mabon DW and Stauffer DH (1976) *Foreign Relations of the United States, 1950, the United Nations; the Western Hemisphere, Volume II.* Washington, D.C.: United States Government Printing Office.

Goscha CE (2006) Courting Diplomatic Disaster? The Difficult Integration of Vietnam into the Internationalist Communist Movement (1945–1950). *Journal of Vietnamese Studies* 1(1–2): 59–103.

Goscha CE (2009) Choosing between the Two Vietnams: 1950 and Southeast Asian Shifts in the International System. In: Goscha CE and Ostermann CF (eds) *Connecting Histories. Decolonization and the Cold War in Southeast Asia, 1945–1962.* Washington, DC: Woodrow Wilson Center Press, pp. 207–237.

Goscha CE (2017) *The Penguin History of Modern Vietnam.* London: Penguin Books.

Graham MW (1933) *The League of Nations and the Recognition of States (Vol. 3).* Berkeley, CA: University of California Press.

Grant TD (1999) *The Recognition of States: Law and Practice in Debate and Evolution.* Westport, CN.; London: Praeger.

Grant TD (2009) *Admission to the United Nations: Charter Article 4 and the Rise of Universal Organization.* Boston: Martinus Nijhoff Publishers.

Gray WG (2003) *Germany's Cold War: The Global Campaign to Isolate East Germany, 1949–1969.* Chapel Hill, N.C.; London: University of North Carolina Press.

Greenhill B (2008) Recognition and Collective Identity Formation in International Politics. *European Journal of International Relations* 14(2): 343–368.

Grewe WG (1979) *Rückblenden: 1976–1951.* Frankfurt am Main: Propyläen.

Grieder P (1998) The Overthrow of Ulbricht in East Germany: A New Interpretation. *Debatte: Journal of Contemporary Central and Eastern Europe* 6(1): 8–45.

Griffiths RD (2017) Admission to the Sovereignty Club: The Past, Present, and Future of the International Recognition Regime. *Territory, Politics, Governance* 5(2): 177–189.

Gu W (1995) *Conflicts of Divided Nations: The Cases of China and Korea.* Westport, CN; London: Praeger.

Haacke J (2005) The Frankfurt School and International Relations: On the Centrality of Recognition. *Review of International Studies* 31(1): 181–194.

Haftendorn H (2006) *Coming of Age: German Foreign Policy since 1945.* Rowman & Littlefield Publishers.

Halliday F (1987) State and Society in International Relations. *Millennium: Journal of International Studies* 16(2): 215–229.

Hallstein-Doktrin Ist Bankrott. (1965) *Neues Deutschland*, March 9, 1965, 1.

Hardt M and Negri A (2000) *Empire*. Cambridge, Massachusetts; London, England: Harvard University Press.

Harrison HM (2003) *Driving the Soviets up the Wall: Soviet-East German Relations, 1953–1961*. Princeton, N.J.: Princeton University Press.

Hechter M (1992) The Dynamics of Secession. *Acta Sociologica* 35(4): 267–283.

Hegel GWF (1991) *Hegel: Elements of the Philosophy of Right*. Cambridge: Cambridge University Press.

Henderson G (1974) Korea. In: Henderson G, Lebow RN and Stoessinger JG (eds) *Divided Nations in a Divided World*. New York: David McKay Company, pp. 43–96.

Henderson G and Lebow RN (1974) Conclusion. In: Henderson G, Lebow RN and Stoessinger JG (eds) *Divided Nations in a Divided World*. New York: David McKay Company, pp. 433–454.

Henderson W and Fishel WR (1966) The Foreign Policy of Ngo Dinh Diem. *Vietnam Perspectives* 2(1): 3–30.

Hentilä S (2014) Finland as the First Target of the Hallstein-Doctrine. In: Rentola K and Saarela T (eds) *Kulkijapoika on Nähnyt Sen: Kirjoituksia Nykyhistoriasta*. Helsinki: Työväen historian ja perinteen tutkimuksen seura, pp. 116–130.

Heping Xieshang De You Yi Zhongda Shengli [Another Great Victory of Peaceful Negotiations]. (1954) *People's Daily*, July 22, 1954, 1.

Herring GC (1996) *America's Longest War: The United States and Vietnam, 1950–1975*. New York: McGraw-Hill.

Himmrich JLA (2016) *Germany's Recognition of Kosovo as an Independent State in 2008*. PhD, London School of Economics and Political Science, London.

Hinsley FH (1967) *Power and the Pursuit of Peace: Theory and Practice in the History of Relations between States*. Cambridge: Cambridge University Press.

Ho CM (1961) *Selected Works: Volume III*. Hanoi: Foreign Languages Publishing House.

Ho CM (1962) *Selected Works: Volume IV*. Hanoi: Foreign Languages Publishing House.

Hobsbawm EJ (2012) *Nations and Nationalism since 1780: Programme, Myth, Reality*. Cambridge, New York: Cambridge University Press.

Hobson C (2008) "Democracy as Civilisation". *Global Society* 22(1): 75–95.

Hobson JM (2013) The Other Side of the Westphalian Frontier. In: Seth S (ed) *Postcolonial Theory and International Relations*. London; New York: Routledge, pp. 32–48.

Hoffmann S (1977) An American Social Science: International Relations. *Daedalus: Journal of the American Academy of Arts and Sciences* 106(3): 41–60.

Hrdlicka MR (1990) The Korean War and the Rearmament of the Federal Republic of Germany. In: Kang M-K and Wagner H (eds) *Korea and Germany: Lessons in Division*. Seoul: Seoul National University Press, pp. 276–301.

Hu S (2015) Small State Foreign Policy: The Diplomatic Recognition of Taiwan. *China: An International Journal* 13(2): 1–23.

Hudson VM and Day BS (2020) *Foreign Policy Analysis: Classic and Contemporary Theory*. Lanham, Boulder, New York, London: Rowman & Littlefield.

Hwang E-G (1993) *The Korean Economies: A Comparison of North and South*. Oxford: Clarendon Press.

Ikenberry GJ (2011) *Liberal Leviathan: The Origins, Crisis, and Transformation of the American World Order*. Princeton: Princeton University Press.

Institut De Droit International (1936) Resolutions Concerning the Recognition of New States and New Governments. *American Journal of International Law* 30(4): 185–187.

Jack HA (1955) *Bandung: An on-the-Spot Description of the Asian-African Conference, Bandung, Indonesia, April 1955*. Chicago: Toward Freedom.

James A (1986) *Sovereign Statehood: The Basis of International Society*. London; Boston; Sydney: Allen and Unwin.

Jiang H (2016) Guo Ji Leng Zhan, Ge Ming Wai Jiao Yu Dui Wai Yuan Zhu: Zhong Guo Dui Fei Yuan Zhu Zheng Ce De Zai Kao Cha, 1956–1965 [Cold War, Revolutionary Diplomacy and Foreign Aid: China's African Aid Policy Revisited, 1956–1965]. *Foreign Affairs Review* 5: 81–108.

Jones H (1999) *Abraham Lincoln and a New Birth of Freedom: The Union and Slavery in the Diplomacy of the Civil War*. Lincoln: University of Nebraska Press.

Jonsson G (2017) *Towards Korean Reconciliation: Socio-Cultural Exchanges and Cooperation*. London: Routledge.

Kahin GM (1956) *The Asian-African Conference: Bandung, Indonesia, April 1955*. New York: Cornell University Press.

Karnow S (1984) *Vietnam: A History*. New York: Penguin Books.

Keefer EC and Mabon DW (1985) *Foreign Relations of the United States, 1955–1957, Volume I, Vietnam*. United States Government Printing Office.

Keefer EC, Mabon DW and Schwar HD (1996) *Foreign Relations of the United States, 1961–1963, Volume Xxii, Northeast Asia*. Washington, D.C.: United States Government Printing Office.

Keene E (2002) *Beyond the Anarchical Society: Grotius, Colonialism and Order in World Politics*. Cambridge: Cambridge University Press.

Kennedy JF (1956) *America's Stake in Vietnam. Speech at the Conference on Vietnam Luncheon, June 1, 1956*. Available at: www.jfklibrary.org/archives/other-resources/john-f-kennedy-speeches/vietnam-conference-washington-dc-1956060 (accessed December 27, 2018).

Kennedy JF (1964) *John F. Kennedy: 1963: Containing the Public Messages, Speeches, and Statements of the Rresident, January 20 to November 22, 1963*. Washington, D.C.: United States Government Printing Office.

Keohane RO (1986) Realism, Neorealism and the Study of World Politics. In: Keohane RO (ed) *Neorealism and Its Critics*. New York: Columbia University Press, pp. 1–26.

Ker-Lindsay J (2012) *The Foreign Policy of Counter Secession: Preventing the Recognition of Contested States*. Oxford: Oxford University Press.

Ker-Lindsay J (2015) Engagement without Recognition: The Limits of Diplomatic Interaction with Contested States. *International Affairs* 91(2): 267–285.

Kilian W (2001) *Die Hallstein-Doktrin: Der Diplomatische Krieg Zwischen Der Brd Und Der Ddr 1955–1973*. Berlin: Duncker & Humblot.

Kim C-H (1970) The United Nations and Dilemmas of Korea Reunification. *The Journal of Asiatic Studies* 13(4): 419–431.

Kim H-J (1977) *The Unification Policy of South and North Korea: A Comparative Study*. Seoul: Seoul National University Press.

Kim IS (1964) *On Eliminating Dogmatism and Formalism and Establishing Jooche in Ideological Work*. Pyongyang: Foreign Languages Publishing House.

Kim K-J (2020) Korean Foreign Policy: A Historical Overview. In: Moon C-I and Moon MJ (eds) *Routledge Handbook of Korean Politics and Public Administration*. Abingdon, Oxon; New York, N.Y.: Routledge, pp. 129–143.

Kirby WC (2001) The Two Chinas in the Global Setting: Sino-Soviet and Sino-American Cooperation in the 1950s. In: Ross RS and Jiang C (eds) *Re-Examining the Cold War. U.S.-China Diplomacy, 1954–1973*. Cambridge, Massachusetts: Harvard University Press, pp. 25–45.

Kitchens AH and Petersen NH (1981) *Foreign Relations of the United States, 1952–1954, Volume Xvi, the Geneva Conference*. Washington, DC: United States Government Printing Office.

Klein D (1963) Formosa's Diplomatic World. *The China Quarterly* 15: 45–50.

Kleuters J (2012) *Reunification in West German Party Politics from Westbindung to Ostpolitik*. Houndmills, Basingstroke, Hampshire, UK: Palgrave Macmillan.

Kolstø P (2006) The Sustainability and Future of Unrecognized Quasi-States. *Journal of Peace Research* 43(6): 723–740.

Krasner SD (1993) Westphalia and All That. In: Goldstein J and Keohane RO (eds) *Ideas and Foreign Policy. Beliefs, Institutions, and Political Change*. Ithaca: Cornell University Press, pp. 235–264.

Krasner SD (1999) *Sovereignty*. Princeton, N.J.: Princeton University Press.

Kreijen G (2004) *State Failure, Sovereignty and Effectiveness: Legal Lessons from the Decolonization of Sub-Saharan Africa*. Leiden: Martinus Nijhoff Publishers.

Kuklick B (1972) *American Policy and the Division of Germany: The Clash with Russia over Reparations*. Ithaca: Cornell University Press.

Kurtulus E (2005) *State Sovereignty: Concept, Phenomenon, and Ramifications*. London: Palgrave Macmillan.

Küsters HJ (1996) *Dokumente Zur Deutschlandpolitik: II. Reihe/Band 2: Die Konstituierung Der Bundesrepublik Deutschland Und Der Deutschen Demokratischen Republik. 7. September Bis 31. Dezember 1949*. München: Oldenbourg.

Lammers KC (2006) Living Next Door to Germany: Denmark and the German Problem. *Contemporary European History* 15(4): 453–472.

Laoutides C (2020) The Ethics of State Recognition. In: Visoka G, Doyle J and Newman E (eds) *Routledge Handbook of State Recognition*. London: Routledge, pp. 59–70.

Larkin BD (1973) *China and Africa 1949–1970: The Foreign Policy of the People's Republic of China*. Berkeley, C.A.: University of California Press.

Lauterpacht H (1947) *Recognition in International Law*. Cambridge: Cambridge University Press.

Lawler P (2005) The Good State: In Praise of "Classical" Internationalism. *Review of International Studies* 31(3): 427–449.

Lee MY (2011) The Vietnam War: South Korea's Search for National Security. In: Kim B-K and Vogel EF (eds) *The Park Chung Hee Era. The Transformation of South Korea*. Cambridge, Massachusetts: Harvard University Press, pp. 403–429.

Lee S and Moon C-I (2020) Korean Unification Policy. In: Moon C-I and Moon MJ (eds) *Routledge Handbook of Korean Politics and Public Administration*. Abingdon, Oxon; New York, NY: Routledge, pp. 177–192.

Li D and Xia Y (2018) *Mao and the Sino-Soviet Split, 1959–1973: A New History*. Lanham; Boulder; New York; London: Lexington Books.

Li X (2018) *The Cold War in East Asia.* London and New York: Routledge Taylor & Francis Group.

Lim J (2014) Confucianism as a Symbol of Solidarity: Cultural Relations between the Republic of China and the Republic of Vietnam, 1955–1963. *Issues and Studies* 50(4): 119–156.

Lin H-T (2013) U.S.-Taiwan Military Diplomacy Revisited: Chiang Kai-Shek, Baituan, and the 1954 Mutual Defense Pact. *Diplomatic History* 37(5): 971–994.

Linklater A (2016) The 'Standard of Civilisation' in World Politics. *Human Figurations* 5(2).

Liu PH (2007) Maintaining US-Republic of China Alliance Via Africa: A Review of the Vanguard Project. *Taiwan Historical Research* 14(2): 161–181.

Liu PH (2012) Beyond Agricultural Assistance: Little China's Big African Illusion. *Taiwan Historical Research* 19(1): 141–171.

Liu W (2014) *China in the United Nations.* Hackensack, N.J.: World Scientific.

Logevall F (1993) The Swedish-American Conflict over Vietnam. *Diplomatic History* 17(3): 421–445.

Loth W (1994) *Stalins Ungeliebtes Kind: Warum Moskau Die DDR Nicht Wollte.* Berlin: Rowohlt.

Luard E (1971) China and the United Nations. *International Affairs* 47(4): 729–744.

Lüthi LM (2008) *The Sino-Soviet Split: Cold War in the Communist World.* Princeton, NJ: Princeton University Press.

Lüthi LM (2014) Rearranging International Relations? How Mao's China and De Gaulle's France Recognized Each Other in 1963–1964. *Journal of Cold War Studies* 16(1): 111–145.

Luu VL (2000) *Fifty Years of Vietnamese Diplomacy, 1945–1995: Volume I: 1945–1975.* Hanoi: The Gioi Publishers.

Mackie J (2010) The Bandung Conference and Afro-Asian Solidarity: Indonesian Aspects. In: Finnane A and McDougall D (eds) *Bandung 1955. Little Histories.* Caulfield, Vic.: Monash University Press, pp. 9–26.

Major P (2010) *Behind the Berlin Wall: East Germany and the Frontiers of Power.* Oxford: Oxford University Press.

Mandelbaum MM (2013) One State – One Nation: The Naturalisation of Nation-State Congruency in IR Theory. *Journal of International Relations and Development* 16(4): 514–538.

Mao Y (2010) When Zhou Enlai Met Gamal Abdel Nasser: Sino-Egyptian Relations and the Bandung Conference. In: Finnane A and McDougall D (eds) *Bandung 1955. Little Histories.* Caulfield, Vic.: Monash University Press, pp. 89–108.

Mao Z (1961) *Selected Works of Mao Tse-Tung: Vol. IV.* Beijing: Foreign Languages Press.

Mao Z (1998) *Mao Zedong on Diplomacy.* Beijing: Foreign Languages Press.

Marcussen M, Risse T, Engelmann-Martin D, et al. (1999) Constructing Europe? The Evolution of French, British and German Nation State Identities. *Journal of European Public Policy* 6(4): 614–633.

Maricic A (2019) *"Lucky That East Germany Also Exists": Yugoslavia between the Federal Republic of Germany and the German Democratic Republic (1955–1968).* Doctoral Dissertation, University of Waterloo, Waterloo.

Marshall MG, Gurr TR and Jaggers K (2014) Polity IV Project: Political Regime Characteristics and Transitions, 1800–2013. *Center for Systemic Peace.*

Maulucci TW (2012) *Adenauer's Foreign Office: West German Diplomacy in the Shadow of the Third Reich.* DeKalb, Illinois: NIU Press.

Mayall J (1990) *Nationalism and International Society.* Cambridge: Cambridge University Press.

Meyer JW, Boli J, Thomas GM, et al. (1997) World Society and the Nation-State. *American Journal of Sociology* 103(1): 144–181.

Miller EG (2004) *Grand Designs: Vision, Power, and Nation Building in America's Alliance with Ngo Dinh Diem, 1954–1960.* Doctoral Dissertation, Harvard University.

Miller EG (2013) *Misalliance: Ngo Dinh Diem, the United States, and the Fate of South Vietnam.* Cambridge, Massachusetts: Harvard University Press.

Miller RG (2000) *To Save a City: The Berlin Airlift.* College Station: Texas A & M University Press.

Ministry of National Unification. Republic of Korea (1996) *White Paper on Korean Unification.* Seoul: Ministry of National Unification. Republic of Korea.

Misra KP (1966) *India's Policy of Recognition of States and Governments.* Bombay: Allied Publishers.

Mitzen J (2016) Ontological Security in World Politics: State Identity and the Security Dilemma. *European Journal of International Relations* 12(3): 341–370.

Montevideo Convention (1933) Convention on Rights and Duties of States. Available at: http://avalon.law.yale.edu/20th_century/intam03.asp (accessed July 5, 2018).

Morgenthau HJ (1973) *Politics among Nations: The Struggle for Power and Peace.* New York: Alfred A. Knopf.

Murphy AB (1996) The Sovereign State System as Political-Territorial Ideal: Historical and Contemporary Considerations. In: Biersteker TJ and

Weber C (eds) *State Sovereignty as Social Construct.* Cambridge: Cambridge University Press, pp. 81–120.

Neumann IB and Welsh JM (1991) The Other in European Self-Definition: An Addendum to the Literature on International Society. *Review of International Studies* 17(4): 327–348.

Neumayer E (2008) Distance, Power and Ideology: Diplomatic Representation in a World of Nation-States. *Area* 40(2): 228–236.

Newman E and Visoka G (2018) The European Union's Practice of State Recognition: Between Norms and Interests. *Review of International Studies* 44(4): 760–786.

Newman K (2007) *Macmillan, Khrushchev and the Berlin Crisis, 1958–1960.* London: Routledge.

Newnham RE (2000) Embassies for Sale: The Purchase of Diplomatic Recognition by West Germany, Taiwan and South Korea. *International Politics* 37(3): 259–283.

Nguyen VH and Phung TM (2010) *65 Years of Vietnam Diplomacy: 1945–2010.* Hanoi: Nxb-Thong-táan.

Niedhart G (2016) Ostpolitik: Transformation through Communication and the Quest for Peaceful Change. *Journal of Cold War Studies* 18(3): 14–59.

Niu J (2013) *Leng Zhan Yu Xin Zhong Guo Wai Jiao De Yuan Qi 1945–1955 [the Cold War and Origin of Diplomacy of People's Republic of China, 1949–1955].* Beijing: She hui ke xue wen xian chu ban she.

Northedge FS (1976) *The International Political System.* London: Faber & Faber.

Obama B (2020) *A Promised Land.* London: Viking.

Oberdorfer D and Carlin R (2013) *The Two Koreas: A Contemporary History.* New York: Basic Books.

Oberländer G (1981) *Dokumente Zur Deutschlandpolitik: IV. Reihe/Band 12: 1. Januar Bis 30. November 1966.* Frankfurt am Main: Alfred Metzner.

Oberländer G (1984) *Dokumente Zur Deutschlandpolitik: V. Reihe/Band 1:1. Dezember 1966 Bis 31. Dezember 1967.* Frankfurt am Main: Alfred Metzner.

Obrist U (2001) *Die Heimliche Anerkennung Südvietnams Durch Die Schweiz: Die Beziehungen Der Schweiz Zum Geteilten Vietnam (1954–1963).* Frauenfeld: Huber.

Oda S (1967) The Normalization of Relations between Japan and the Republic of Korea. *American Journal of International Law* 61: 35–56.

Olsen EA (2005) *Korea, the Divided Nation.* Westport, Connecticut; London: Praeger.

Olsen M (2007) *Soviet-Vietnam Relations and the Role of China 1949–64: Changing Alliance.* London: Routledge.

Onuf N (1994) The Constitution of International Society. *European Journal of International Law* 5(1): 1–19.

Oppenheim L (1955) *International Law: A Treatise. Vol.1, Peace.* London: Longman's Green and Co.

Orlow D (2006) The Gdr's Failed Search for a National Identity, 1945–1989. *German Studies Review* 29(3): 537–558.

Osiander A (2001) Sovereignty, International Relations, and the Westphalian Myth. *International Organization* 55(2): 251–287.

Papers Relating to the Foreign Relations of the United States, with the Annual Message of the President Transmitted to Congress December 3, 1907, Part II. (1910) Washington, D.C.: United States Government Printing Office.

Park HS (2002) *North Korea: The Politics of Unconventional Wisdom.* Boulder, Colorado: Lynne Rienner Publishing.

Patil V (2008) *Negotiating Decolonization in the United Nations: Politics of Space, Identity, and International Community.* New York: Routledge.

Payne RJ and Veney CR (2001) Taiwan and Africa: Taipei's Continuing Search for International Recognition. *African and Asian Studies* 36(4): 437–450.

Pegg S (2017) Twenty Years of De Facto State Studies: Progress, Problems, and Prospects. In: Pegg S (ed) *Oxford Research Encyclopedia of Politics.* Oxford: Oxford University Press.

Petersen NH, Slany WZ, Sampson CS, et al. (1976) *Foreign Relations of the United States, 1950, Volume VI, East Asia and the Pacific.* Washington, D.C.: United States Government Printing Office.

Peterson MJ (1982) Political Use of Recognition: The Influence of the International System. *World Politics* 34(3): 324–352.

Peterson MJ (1997) *Recognition of Governments: Legal Doctrine and State Practice, 1815–1995.* Basingstoke: Macmillan.

Peterson MJ (2006) *The UN General Assembly.* London: Routledge.

Pham VD (1955) *Our Struggle in the Past and at Present.* Hanoi: Foreign Languages Publishing House.

Poplai SL (1955) *Selected Documents of the Bandung Conference: Texts of Selected Speeches and Final Communique of the Asian-African Conference, Bandung, Indonesia, Apr. 18–24, 1955.* New York: Institute of Pacific Relations.

Press and Information Department VMoFA (2013) *Danh Sach Cac Nuoc Co Quan He Ngoai Giao Voi Nuoc Chxhcn Viet Nam [List of Countries Which*

Maintains Diplomatic Relations with the Socialist Republic of Vietnam]. Available at: www.mofa.gov.vn/vi/cn_vakv (accessed February 1, 2019).

Radchenko S and Schaefer B (2017) 'Red on White': Kim Il Sung, Park Chung Hee, and the Failure of Korea's Reunification, 1971–1973. *Cold War History* 17(3): 259–277.

Reid JG (1975) *Foreign Relations of the United States, 1949, Volume VII, Part 1 the Far East and Australasia.* Washington, D.C.: United States Government Printing Office.

Reid JG and Glennon JP (1976) *Foreign Relations of the United States, 1949, the Far East and Australasia, Volume VII, Part 2.* Washington, D.C.: United States Government Printing Office.

Reid JG and Stauffer DH (1974) *Foreign Relations of the United States, 1948, the Far East and Australasia, Volume VI.* Washington, D.C.: United States Government Printing Office.

Republic of Vietnam (1961) *The Problem of Reunification of Vietnam.* Saigon: Nha in Thong Tin.

Rhee KS (1993) Korea's Unification: The Applicability of the German Experience. *Asian Survey* 33(4): 360–375.

Rich TS (2009) Status for Sale: Taiwan and the Competition for Diplomatic Recognition. *Issues and Studies* 45(4): 159–188.

Rich TS and Banerjee V (2015) Running out of Time? The Evolution of Taiwan's Relations in Africa. *Journal of Current Chinese Affairs* 44(1): 141–161.

Richards R and Smith R (2015) Playing in the Sandbox: State Building in the Space of Non-Recognition. *Third World Quarterly* 36(9): 1717–1735.

Ringmar E (1996) On the Ontological Status of the State. *European Journal of International Relations* 2(4): 439–466.

Ringmar E (2002) The Recognition Game: Soviet Russia against the West. *Cooperation & Conflict* 37(2): 115–136.

Ringmar E (2012) The International Politics of Recognition. In: Lindemann T and Ringmar E (eds) *The International Politics of Recognition.* Boulder, Colo.: Paradigm, pp. 3–23.

Ringmar E (2014) Recognition and the Origins of International Society. *Global Discourse* 4(4): 446–458.

Rintz WA (2009) The Failure of the China White Paper. *Constructing the Past* 11(1): 76–84.

Ruggenthaler P (2015) *The Concept of Neutrality in Stalin's Foreign Policy, 1945–1953.* Lanham: Lexington Books.

Rupieper H-J (1986) Die Berliner Außenministerkonferenz Von 1954. Ein Höhepunkt Der Ost-West-Propaganda Oder Die Letzte Möglichkeit Zur Schaffung Der Deutschen Einheit? *Vierteljahrshefte für Zeitgeschichte* 34(3): 427–453.

Russett B (1994) *Grasping the Democratic Peace*. Princeton: Princeton University Press.

Ryngaert C and Sobrie S (2011) Recognition of States: International Law or Realpolitik? The Practice of Recognition in the Wake of Kosovo, South Ossetia, and Abkhazia. *Leiden Journal of International Law* 24(2): 467–490.

Said EW (1993) *Culture and Imperialism*. London: Chatto & Windus.

Sappington NO, Glennon JP, Kent GO, et al. (1967) *Foreign Relations of the United States: Diplomatic Papers, 1945, General: Political and Economic Matters, Volume II*. Washington, D.C.: United States Government Printing Office.

Sarotte ME (2001) *Dealing with the Devil: East Germany, Détente, and Ostpolitik, 1969–1973*. Chapel Hill: University of North Carolina Press.

Saxer CJ (2017) The Korea Question and the Nordic Response: From War Participation to Diplomatic Recognition. *Korea Journal* 57(1): 128–152.

Scalapino RA (1963) The Foreign Policy of North Korea. *The China Quarterly* 14: 30–50.

Schaufelbuehl JM, Wyss M and Bott S (2015) Choosing Sides in the Global Cold War: Switzerland, Neutrality, and the Divided States of Korea and Vietnam. *The International History Review* 37(5): 1014–1036.

Schmidt H-I (2003) Pushed to the Front: The Foreign Assistance Policy of the Federal Republic of Germany, 1958–1971. *Contemporary European History* 12(4): 473–507.

Scholz MF (2006) East Germany's North European Policy Prior to International Recognition of the German Democratic Republic. *Contemporary European History* 15(4): 553–571.

Schwabe K (1991) German Policy Responses to the Marshall Plan. In: Maier CS (ed) *The Marshall Plan and Germany. West German Development within the Framework of the European Recovery Program*. New York: Berg, pp. 225–281.

Schwar HD (1998) *Foreign Relations of the United States, 1964–1968, Volume XXX, China*. Washington, D.C.: United States Government Printing Office.

Selvage D (2004) Poland, the GDR, and the "Ulbricht Doctrine". In: Biskupski MBB (ed) *Ideology, Politics, and Diplomacy in East Central Europe*. Rochester, N.Y.: University of Rochester Press, pp. 227–241.

Shaw MN (2017) *International Law*. Cambridge: Cambridge University Press.

Shelef NG and Zeira Y (2017) Recognition Matters! *Journal of Conflict Resolution* 61(3): 537–563.

Shen Z (2004) *Mao Zedong, Sidalin Yu Chaoxian Zhan Zheng [Mao Zedong, Stalin, and the Korean War]*. Guangzhou: Guangdong ren min chu ban she.

Shinn DH and Eisenman J (2012) *China and Africa: A Century of Engagement*. Philadelphia: University of Pennsylvania Press.

Smith T (1994) *America's Mission: The United States and the Worldwide Struggle for Democracy in the Twentieth Century*. Princeton, N.J.: Princeton University Press.

Spilker D (2006) *The East German Leadership and the Division of Germany: Patriotism and Propaganda 1945–1953*. Oxford: Clarendon.

Spruyt H (1994) *The Sovereign State and Its Competitors: An Analysis of Systems Change*. Princeton, N.J.: Princeton University Press.

Staadt J (1993) *Die Geheime Westpolitik Der SED 1960–1970: Von Der Gesamtdeutschen Orientierung Zur Sozialistischen Nation*. Berlin: Akademie Verlag.

Stanciu C (2014) Autonomy and Ideology: Brezhnev, Ceauşescu and the World Communist Movement. *Contemporary European History* 23(1): 115–134.

Stauffer DH, Sampson CS, Rose LA, et al. (1977) *Foreign Relations of the United States, 1950, Western Europe, Volume III*. Washington, D.C.: United States Government Printing Office.

Sterio M (2013) *The Right to Self-Determination under International Law: 'Selfistans', Secession, and the Rule of the Great Powers*. London: Routledge.

Sterio M (2020) Power Politics and State Recognition. In: Visoka G, Doyle J and Newman E (eds) *Routledge Handbook of State Recognition*. London: Routledge, pp. 82–98.

Stivachtis YA (2015) Liberal Democracy, Market Economy, and International Conduct as Standards of "Civilization" in Contemporary International Society: The Case of Russia's Entry into the "Community of Civilized States". *Journal of Eurasian Studies* 6(2): 130–142.

Strang D (1991) Anomaly and Commonplace in European Political Expansion: Realist and Institutional Accounts. *International Organization* 45(2): 143–162.

Subotić J (2016) Narrative, Ontological Security, and Foreign Policy Change. *Foreign Policy Analysis* 12(4): 610–627.

Sufott EZ (2007) Israel's China Policy 1950–92. *Israel Affairs* 7(1): 94–118.

Suh D-S (1988) *Kim Il Sung: The North Korean Leader*. New York: Columbia University Press.

Susskind J (2018) *Future Politics: Living Together in a World Transformed by Tech.* Oxford: Oxford University Press.

Szalontai B (2018) The "Sole Legal Government of Vietnam": The Bao Dai Factor and Soviet Attitudes toward Vietnam, 1947–1950. *Journal of Cold War Studies* 20(3): 3–56.

Taylor J (2009) *The Generalissimo: Chiang Kai-Shek and the Struggle for Modern China.* Cambridge, Massachusetts: Belknap Press of Harvard University Press.

Thayer NB (1974) China: The Formosa Question. In: Henderson G, Lebow RN and Stoessinger JG (eds) *Divided Nations in a Divided World.* New York: David McKay Company, pp. 99–126.

Thien TT (1963) *India and South East Asia, 1947–1960.* Genève: Droz.

Thomaneck JKA and Niven B (2001) *Dividing and Uniting Germany.* London: Routledge.

Tilly C (1975) Reflections on the History of European State-Making. In: Tilly C (ed) *The Formation of National States in Western Europe.* Princeton, N.J.: Princeton University Press, pp. 3–83.

Tran N-A (2013) *Contested Identities: Nationalism in the Republic of Vietnam (1954–1963).* Doctoral Dissertation, University of California, Berkeley.

Trentin M (2009) Modernization as State Building: The Two Germanies in Syria, 1963–1972. *Diplomatic History* 33(3): 487–505.

Troche A (1996) *Ulbricht Und Die Dritte Welt: Ost-Berlins "Kampf" Gegen Die Bonner "Alleinvertretungsanmassung".* Erlangen: Palm und Enke.

Tucker NB (1983) *Patterns in the Dust: Chinese-American Relations and the Recognition Controversy, 1949–1950.* New York: Columbia University Press.

Turns D (2003) The Stimson Doctrine of Non-Recognition: Its Historical Genesis and Influence on Contemporary International Law. *Chinese Journal of International Law* 2(1): 105–143.

United Nations (1945) Charter of the United Nations. Available at: https://www.un.org/en/sections/un-charter/un-charter-full-text/ (accessed July 3, 2020).

United Nations (1950) *Yearbook of the United Nations, 1948–49.* Department of Public Information, United Nations.

United Nations (1956) *Treaty Series: Treaties and International Agreements Registered or Filed and Recorded with the Secretariat of the United Nations.* New York.

United Nations (1968) *Treaty Series: Treaties and International Agreements Registered or Filed and Recorded with the Secretariat of the United Nations.* New York.

United Nations General Assembly (1948) *The Problem of the Independence of Korea*. A/RES/195(III), available from undocs.org/en/A/RES/195(III).

United Nations General Assembly (1951) *Intervention of the Central People's Government of the People's Republic of China in Korea*. A/RES/498(V), available from undocs.org/en/A/RES/498(V).

United Nations General Assembly (1960) *Declaration on the Granting of Independence to Colonial Countries and Peoples*. A/RES/1514(XV), available from undocs.org/en/A/Res/1514(XV).

United Nations General Assembly (1961a) *Admission of the Mongolian People's Republic to Membership in the United Nations*. A/RES/1630(XVI), available from undocs.org/en/A/Res/1630(XVI).

United Nations General Assembly (1961b) *Representation of China in the United Nations*. A/RES/1668(XVI), available from undocs.org/en/A/Res/1668(XVI).

United Nations General Assembly (1971) *Restoration of the Lawful Rights of the People's Republic of China in the United Nations*. A/RES/2758(XXVI), available from undocs.org/en/A/Res/12758(XXVI).

United Nations Security Council (1949) Official Records Fourth Year, No. 13. U.N. Doc. S/PV. 410, available from undocs.org/S/PV.410.

United Nations Security Council (1950) *Complaint of Aggression Upon the Republic of Korea*. S/RES/83(1950), available from undocs.org/en/S/Res/83(1950).

United States Department of States (1985) *Documents on Germany: 1944–1985*. Washington, D.C.: United States Government Printing Office.

United States. Department of Defense (1971) *United States – Vietnam Relations 1945–1967*. Washington, D.C.: United States Government Printing Office.

United States. Department of State (1949) *The Department of State Bulletin: Vol. XX, No. 496*. Washington, D.C.: United States Government Printing Office.

United States. Department of State (1950) *The Department of State Bulletin: Vol. XXIII, No. 574*. Washington, D.C.: United States Government Printing Office.

United States. Department of State (1960) *The Record on Korean Unification, 1943–1960: Narrative Summary with Principal Documents*. Washington, D.C.: United States Government Printing Office.

Unvereinbar Mit Völkerrecht: Ministerium Für Auswärtige Angelegenheiten Der DDR Zur Jüngsten Bonner Erpressung Gegen Jugoslawien. (1957) *Neues Deutschland*, October 20, 1957, 1.

Van Fossen A (2007) The Struggle for Recognition: Diplomatic Competition between China and Taiwan in Oceania. *Journal of Chinese Political Science* 12(2): 125–146.

Van Ness P (2018) China as a Third World State: Foreign Policy and Official National Identity. In: Dittmer L and Kim SS (eds) *China's Quest for National Identity*. Ithaca, NY: Cornell University Press, pp. 194–214.

Vidmar J (2009) International Legal Responses to Kosovo's Declaration of Independence. *Vanderbilt Journal of Transnational Law* 42: 779–851.

Vietnam National Archives Center II (1960) V/V Quan He Giua Viet Nam Voi Mali Nam 1960 [Regarding the Relations between Vietnam and Mali in 1960]. DICH No. 9108.

Vietnam National Archives Center II (1961) V/V Quan He Giua Viet Nam Voi Nam Duong Nam 1961 [Regarding the Relations between Vietnam and Indonesia in 1961]. DICH No. 9205.

Vietnam National Archives Center II (1962) V/V Quan He Giua Viet Nam Va Ai Lao Nam 1962 [Regarding the Relations between Vietnam and Laos in 1962]. DICH No. 9293.

von Bressensdorf AB and Seefried E (2017) Introduction: West Germany and the Global South in the Cold War Era. In: von Bressensdorf AB, Ostermann C and Seefried E (eds) *West Germany, the Global South and the Cold War*. Munich: De Gruyter Oldenbourg, pp. 7–24.

Von Glahn G and Taulbee JL (2017) *Law among Nations: An Introduction to Public International Law*. New York: Routledge.

Vu T (2009) From Cheering to Volunteering: Vietnamese Communists and the Coming of the Cold War, 1940–1951. In: Goscha CE and Ostermann CF (eds) *Connecting Histories. Decolonization and the Cold War in Southeast Asia, 1945–1962*. Washington, D.C.: Woodrow Wilson Center Press, pp. 172–206.

Wagner EW (1961) Failure in Korea. *Foreign Affairs* 40: 128–135.

Wallerstein IM (2004) *World-Systems Analysis: An Introduction*. Durham: Duke University Press.

Waltz KN (1979) *Theory of International Politics*. Reading, Mass.: Addison-Wesley.

Waltz KN (1986) Reflections on Theory of International Politics: A Response to My Critics. In: Keohane RO (ed) *Neorealism and Its Critics*. New York: Columbia University Press, pp. 322–345.

Wang B (1985) *Zhong Mei Huitan Jiunian Huigu [Nine Years Sino-American Talks in Retrospect]*. Beijing: Shi jie zhi shi chu ban she.

Wang T (2017) Neutralizing Indochina: The 1954 Geneva Conference and China's Efforts to Isolate the United States. *Journal of Cold War Studies* 19(2): 3–42.

Wang W-L (2009) The Diplomatic Competition between the ROC Government and the PRC Government in Dahomey (1964–1966). *Bulletin of Academia Historica* 21: 151–190.

Watson A (1984) European International Society and Its Expansion. In: Bull H and Watson A (eds) *The Expansion of International Society*. Oxford: Clarendon Press, pp. 13–32.

Watson A (1992) *The Evolution of International Society: A Comparative Historical Analysis*. London: Routledge.

Wei L-T (1978) *Africa and the Two Chinas*. Doctoral Dissertation, Oklahoma State University.

Weidmann NB, Kuse D and Gleditsch KS (2010) The Geography of the International System: The CShapes Dataset. *International Interactions* 36(1): 86–106.

Wendt AE (1992) Anarchy Is What States Make of It: The Social Construction of Power Politics. *International Organization* 46(2): 391–425.

Wendt AE (1999) *Social Theory of International Politics*. Cambridge: Cambridge University Press.

Wendt AE (2003) Why a World State Is Inevitable. *European Journal of International Relations* 9(4): 491–542.

Wert D, Oh JJ and Kim I (2016) DPRK Diplomatic Relations. Report: The National Commitee on North Korea.

Westad OA (2005) *The Global Cold War: Third World Interventions and the Making of Our Times*. Cambridge: Cambridge University Press.

Westad OA (2017) *The Cold War: A World History*. London: Allen Lane.

Wight M (1977) *Systems of States*. Leicester: Leicester University Press.

Wilson JR and Lorenz KA (2015) *Modeling Binary Correlated Responses Using SAS, SPSS and R*. Heidelberg; New York; Dordrecht; London: Springer.

Winrow GM (1990) *The Foreign Policy of the GDR in Africa*. Cambridge: Cambridge University Press.

Xinhua News Agency (1989) *China's Foreign Relations: A Chronology of Events (1949–1988)*. Beijing: Foreign Languages Press.

Yan X (2020) Xin Guan Fei Yan Yi Qing Wei Qu Quan Qiu Hua Ti Gong He Li Xing [the Covid-19 Pandemic Provides Rational for Deglobalizaiton]. *Quarterly Journal of International Politics* 5(3): III–VI.

Yang K (2009) *Zhonghua Renmin Gongheguo Jian Guo Shi Yan Jiu 2 [Research on the History of the Founding of the People's Republic of China 2]*. Nanchang: Jiangxi ren min chu ban she.

Yang W-C (2011) Lu Han Yu Zhong Fa Yue Nan Jiao She 1945–1946 [Lu Han and the Negotiations over Vietnam between China and France, 1945–1946]. *Archives Quarterly* 10(1): 16–27.

Yang Y-F (1997) *Der Alleinvertretungsanspruch Der Geteilten Länder: Deutschland, Korea Und China Im Politischen Vergleich.* Frankfurt am Main: Lang.

Yemelianova GM (2015) Western Academic Discourse on the Post-Soviet De Facto State Phenomenon. *Caucasus Survey* 3(3): 219–238.

Young B (2015) The Struggle for Legitimacy: North Korea's Relations with Africa, 1965–1992. *European Journal of Korean Studies* 16: 97–116.

Yu GT (1977) China and the Third World. *Asian Survey* 17(11): 1036–1048.

Zarakol A (2011) *After Defeat: How the East Learned to Live with the West.* Cambridge: Cambridge University Press.

Zhai Q (2012) From Estrangement to Normalization: Sino-French Relations in 1949–1964. *CCP History Studies* 8: 14–27.

Zhang Q (2014) Towards an Integrated Theory of Chinese Foreign Policy: Bringing Leadership Personality Back In. *Journal of Contemporary China* 23(89): 902–922.

Zhang SG (2007) Constructing 'Peaceful Coexistence': China's Diplomacy toward the Geneva and Bandung Conferences, 1954–55. *Cold War History* 7(4): 509–528.

Zhang X (2010) A Rising China and the Normative Changes in International Society. *East Asia* 28(3): 235–246.

Zhang Y (1991) China's Entry into International Society: Beyond the Standard of 'Civilization'. *Review of International Studies* 17(1): 3–16.

Zhong gong zhong yang wen xian yan jiu shi (1997) *Zhou Enlai Nian Pu, 1949–1976 [A Chronicle of Zhou Enlai's Life: 1949–1976].* Beijing: Zhong yang wen xian chu ban she.

Zhou E (1949) Telegram Addressed to the Secrectary-General. Beijing.

Zuo Y (2012) Self-Identificaiton, Recognition, and Conflicts: The Evolution of Taiwan's Identity, 1949–2008. In: Lindemann T and Ringmar E (eds) *The International Politics of Recognition.* Boulder, Colo.: Paradigm, pp. 153–169.

www.ingramcontent.com/pod-product-compliance
Lightning Source LLC
Chambersburg PA
CBHW031541260326
41914CB00002B/207